W9-BMU-752

MYTHOLOGY AND CULTURE WORLDWIDE

Norse Mythology

SHIRLEY-RAYE REDMOND

LUCENT BOOKS

A part of Gale, Cengage Learning

GALE
CENGAGE Learning

Detroit • New York • San Francisco • New Haven, Conn • Waterville, Maine • London

GALE
CENGAGE Learning·

LIBRARY OF CONGRESS CATALOGING-IN-PUBLICATION DATA

Redmond, Shirley-Raye, 1955-
  Norse mythology / by Shirley-Raye Redmond.
     p. cm. -- (Mythology and culture worldwide)
  Includes bibliographical references (p.   ) and index.
  ISBN 978-1-4205-0717-1 (hardcover)
  1. Mythology, Norse--Juvenile literature. I. Title.
  BL860.R4155 2012
  293'.13--dc23

                                                              2012002940

Lucent Books
27500 Drake Rd.
Farmington Hills, MI 48331

ISBN-13: 978-1-4205-0717-1
ISBN-10: 1-4205-0717-6

Printed in the United States of America
2 3 4 5 6 7 16 15 14 13 12

TABLE OF CONTENTS

Map of Scandinavia

Genealogy of Major Norse Gods, Giants, and Monsters

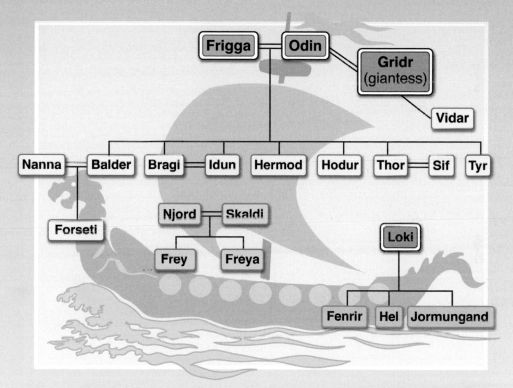

Note: Double lines joining two names indicate that these gods had offspring together.
• Blue shading denotes Aesir gods.
• Green shading denotes Vanir.
• Purple shading denotes giants.

Major Characters in Norse Mythology

Character Name	Pronunciation	Description
Aesir	AY-seer	Chief gods of Asgard.
Balder	BALD-ur	God of goodness and light; son of Odin and Frigga.
Bragi	BRAY-gee	God of poetry and eloquence; son of Odin and Frigga.
Embla	EM-blah	First woman; created by Odin.
Fenrir	FEN-rear	Monstrous wolf; offspring of Loki.
Forseti	FOR-set-ee	Son of Balder and Nana.
Frey	fray	God of fertility; son of Njord and Freya's twin brother.
Freya	FRAY-yah	Fertility goddess; daughter of Njord and Frey's twin sister.
Frigga	frig; rhymes with fig	Queen of the gods.
Heimdall	HAME-doll	God of the dawn.
Hel	hell	Queen of the underworld.
Hodur	HA-dur; rhymes with hotter	Balder's blind brother; son of Odin and Frigga.
Idun	EE-dune	Goddess of youth and beauty; wife of Bragi.
Jormungand	YOR-mun-gand	Giant serpent.
Loki	LOW-key	Giant of mischief and evil.
Mjolnir	MYAWL-nir	Thor's hammer.
Odin	OH-din	Ruler of the gods.
Nanna	NAN-uh; rhymes with Anna	Balder's wife.
Njord	n-YARD	God of the sea.
Sigyn	SEE-gin	Loki's wife.
Thor	thor	God of thunder; son of Odin and Frigga.
Tyr	teer; rhymes with deer	God of war; son of Odin either with Frigga or with an angry giantess.
Uller	OO-ler	God of winter.
Valkyries	val-KEER-eez	Odin's warrior maidens.
Ymir	EE-mair	A brutal frost giant.

Land of the Far North

Norse mythology is a fascinating world of gods and heroes, monsters and giants, love and courage, and combat and death that came from Europe's northernmost regions, the area now home to the Scandinavian countries of Norway, Sweden, Denmark, and Iceland. Like other myths from around the world, the stories of the Norse reflect the culture's spiritual foundations. The tales attempt to explain the origins of the universe; natural phenomena, such as storms and seasonal changes; and what happens to people after they die. In addition, according to author Donna Rosenberg, the purpose of myths is "to instruct members of the community in the attitudes and behavior necessary to function successfully in that particular culture."[1]

The ancient Nordic culture was a complex one. The people were warriors and farmers, pirates and explorers. They were experienced traders as well. Many became wealthy selling furs, walrus tusks, and polar bear skins to the kings and noblemen of Europe. A fiercely independent people, the Norsemen thought nothing of taking whole villages as captives for slave labor. Some Norsemen were master craftsmen who used wood, gold, silver, and stone to create works of art that have survived to this day. While the women had no voice in the political and legal assemblies, they were often

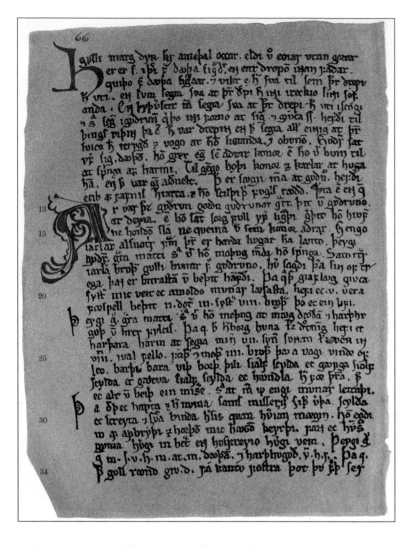

left in charge of farms and fishing businesses while their husbands were gone for months, or even years, on raiding or trading expeditions.

Storytelling was another important part of early Norse culture. Norse myths began as memorized tales that were passed down for centuries from one generation of storytellers to another. Eventually, in the thirteenth century, the stories were put in writing, mainly in Iceland. The Norse greatly admired their poet-storytellers, called skalds, who wrote and related the heroic exploits of gods and courageous warriors.

The Norse gods lived in a glorious city of golden palaces called Asgard. Odin was the most important god in the

Norse pantheon, along with his son Thor, the god of thunder; Frey, the god of fertility; and Frey's twin sister, Freya. Odin was a somber deity who demanded both human and animal sacrifice. His wife Frigga was the queen of the gods. Her son Balder was the god of goodness and light. Bragi was the god of poetry; Tyr was the god of war. Valiant Hermod served as the messenger of the gods. The Norse also believed in a grim underworld ruled by cruel giants. Loki was the most evil of the giants and full of harmful mischief. His daughter Hel was queen of Niflheim, the dark realm of the dishonored dead. Evil Frost Giants were a constant threat to both men and gods.

Among the written sources available for these stories is the *Elder Edda*, sometimes called the *Poetic Edda*. This is a collection of adventure tales, mainly about the hero Sigurd (Siegfried), the dragon slayer. The *Elder Edda* also has poems about the creation of the universe and Ragnarok, the doomsday battle during which all the gods of golden Asgard die. Although written down between A.D. 1000 and 1100, scholars do not know who wrote the poems. Some scholars assume they are a collection of minstrel poems made up by many men and passed down orally from one singer to another for many centuries.

Another written source for Norse myths is the *Younger Edda*, written in the 1200s by an Icelandic historian, poet, and courtier named Snorri Sturluson (1179–1241). It is sometimes called the *Prose Edda*. It relates information about the major Norse deities and provides advice and writing techniques for aspiring poets.

Today, the tales of Odin, Thor, and other Norse gods are often associated with the Vikings, the fearsome sea raiders that plundered coastal settlements throughout Europe and as far as North America during the ninth through twelfth centuries A.D. But the mythology of the Norse existed long before the Vikings ruled the seas. Some scholars believe it may go back as far as the Scandinavian Bronze Age, which lasted for over a thousand years between 1600 and 450 B.C. Archaeologists have found depictions of the Norse gods and goddesses in the fine metal and stone relics dated during that time period.

However old its origins may be, Norse mythology and culture have influenced English customs, language, literature, and laws. In fact, the English word *law* comes from an Old Norse word. Not coincidentally, the annual Norse law assembly, during which laws were passed and disputes settled, was called to order on a Thursday, the day of the week dedicated to Thor. Trolls, ogres, gnomes, elves, and dwarfs—common in the mythology of northern Europe—have long been a part of the English heritage of fairy tales. Many English words, such as *husband, sky, anger, low, window, take, ugly, die, beer, anchor*, and *happy*, have Scandinavian origins. Even *Beowulf*, the first epic poem written by an Anglo-Saxon poet, was inspired by the adventures of heroic Norsemen.

CHAPTER 1

A Cold, Harsh World

The Nordic peoples were descended from indigenous peoples, such as the Samis, who lived in the region during the Scandinavian Bronze Age, and Germanic tribes who moved to northern Europe over two thousand years ago. At the end of the first century A.D., a Roman historian named Tacitus wrote about northern Europe's Germanic, or Teutonic, peoples and their heroic poetry and myths. He reported how they lived in small warrior tribes with kingly leaders and that their first loyalty was to their king, then family, then friends. Retribution—or punishment considered to be fully deserved—often dominated their society. Individuals and families administered justice. The one who was to be punished—and often killed—was expected to face his fate with unflinching courage. Because there was no forgiveness, blood vengeance feuds between the families and clans often continued from one generation to the next. Tacitus noted that these fierce warrior tribes were always on the move, looking for new lands to conquer and for heroic adventures. They settled in areas we now know as Norway, Sweden, Denmark, and Iceland. Moving to the southeast, they conquered the Slavs and Balts and captured important waterways that connect the Baltic and Black Seas. Known as the Rus, or Varangians, they even captured the town of Kiev.

Nordic Settlers in France

In the year 911 a Viking chieftain named Hrolf was granted a portion of land in northern France by the French king. The region was called Normandy and the people called Normans. They went on to conquer Britain and sections of Italy.

These settlers became known to the rest of Europe as the Norse, and then later, as Vikings.

The Nordic tribes continued moving around, always looking for better farmland with less-brutal winters and more fertile soil for growing plentiful crops. Many scholars point out that the geography and climate of northern Europe played a large role in the development of the Norse myths. The rugged landscape, the cold and icy winters, the gleam of the midnight sun, the aurora borealis, and even the ocean—sometimes mild and blue and at other times fierce and lashing—are reflected in the personalities of the major Norse deities, or gods.

The gods of Norse mythology also reflect the characteristics of the people of northern Europe and their culture. The deities speak and behave like Norsemen. They face the same challenges and hardships, such as the dangers of hunting and fishing in cold, icy winters or falling prey to wild animals such as wolves. The gods are susceptible to injury and death. Like the Viking warriors who worshipped them, the gods of Asgard choose to die in battle against their enemies, hoping to make the world a better place for future generations. The gods and goddesses, like the men and women of northern Europe, accept their harsh fate with courageous dignity.

Except for Odin, who occasionally would come to the assistance of a deserving hero, the Norse gods usually do not meddle in human affairs or favor one person over another, as the Greek gods frequently do in the ancient Greek myths. Odin and his sons are somber and often fierce. Although they dwell in Asgard, a city of magnificent palaces, they are constantly on guard against attacks from fierce giants, fiery dragons, and other monsters. The Norse deities are too busy with their own survival to concern themselves with the problems of the people who worship them.

Norse mythology includes many stories of war, battles, and awe-inspiring heroism against dragons and other monsters. The gods and goddesses in the stories are divided

Odin, the supreme Norse god, and his sons were constantly on guard against attacks from fierce giants, fiery dragons, and other monsters.

into two categories: the Aesir, the most exalted of the Norse gods, and the Vanir, the gods of fertility and earthly plenty. Their sworn enemies, such as Loki, are Frost Giants. Neither the Aesir nor Vanir are as carefree as the Greek gods and goddesses, who live a leisurely existence on sunny Mount Olympus, and whose troubles are mostly of their own making.

Death and Lost Causes

Asgard, the dwelling place of the gods, is very unlike the Christian idea of heaven. There is no eternal joy. It is not peaceful. Despite its many splendid palaces, Asgard is a solemn place. The divine residents are forever on the alert, fearing that their enemies—undetected—might cross the rainbow bridge that connects Asgard to the other realms and slay them as they sleep. Those humans lucky enough to make it there in the afterlife have no promise of bliss and eternal joy. Nor are the Norse gods immortal and invincible in the same way that Zeus and Poseidon and Athena are. Norse gods can be seriously injured. They can die, as did the handsome Balder, the best-loved of the Norse gods. They reign in Asgard fully aware that eventually the Frost Giants will destroy their golden city; their palaces will crumble to ruin. Odin, having tasted the magic waters of the Well of Wisdom, has forseen their sad future. They rise each morning, accepting the grim fact that no matter how mightily they try, they will eventually lose.

The Nordic people reasoned that if the future held such a grim outlook for the gods, life on Earth could offer nothing better. A difficult life and death were inevitable. They accepted the fact that if Odin and Thor and Frey would be helpless against the onslaught of evil, so would they. No matter how clever and courageous they tried to be, they could not save themselves. And yet, like their courageous gods, they refused to yield to the evil forces. The ongoing battle between good and evil would never cease until that fateful day when the battle for the end of the world would take place.

Theirs was a lost cause, which led the people of northern Europe to adopt a very sobering worldview called fatalism. This is a stern outlook on life—as harsh as the northern landscape in winter. As historian Edith Hamilton points out, "This is the conception of life which underlies the Norse religion, as somber a conception as the mind of man has ever given birth to . . . the one pure unsullied good [that] men can hope to attain is heroism; and heroism depends on lost causes."[2]

The men of northern Europe believed that the best they could achieve in life was a heroic death. For the Norse, a courageous death was a victory, not defeat. This belief is reflected time and again in both the myths about the gods and the tales and sagas of actual Nordic kings and heroes. The Norsemen, then, naturally valued warfare as the most honorable occupation and courage as the greatest virtue. One of the most frightening and disgusting ideas to the ancient Norsemen was to die a "straw death"—the term they used for dying of disease or old age. Kings and warriors expected to die suddenly and violently, with their swords in their hands. To pass away peacefully in their bed from old age was considered a disgrace.

Odin was the god of victory in battle. Young men early in their lives pledged to live for Odin and vowed to die with their swords in their hands. They dreamed of dying valiantly in battle and being carried to Valhalla, the palace of the slain, by one of the golden-haired Valkyries on their thundering

An illustration of the destruction of Asgard, which Norsemen thought was the dwelling place of their gods.

Valhalla: Warriors' Paradise

The Norse warriors who died heroically in battle hoped to spend their afterlife as guests of Odin in Valhalla. Author H.R. Ellis Davidson describes this Norse warriors' paradise. Valhalla itself "is described as being filled with shields and mailcoats, haunted by wolf and eagle, and provided with hundreds of doors through which the warriors could pour out at any threat of attack."

Warriors who honored Odin in their lives and died heroically in battle "feasted on pork that never gave out, and on mead which flowed instead of milk from the udders of the goat Heidrun. . . . Odin's guests spent the day in fighting, and all who fell in combat were raised again in the evening to feast with the rest."

H.R. Ellis Davidson. *Gods and Myths of Northern Europe.* New York: Penguin, 1964, pp. 149, 28.

This carved stone from the ninth century depicts heroic fallen warriors on their way to Valhalla, the afterlife.

white stallions. They would die fighting because a brave death entitled them to live in Valhalla, the palace of heroes. There they would feast with the gods at night and battle the Frost Giants during the day. According to classics scholar Hamilton, "All the best Northern tales are tragic, about men and women who go steadfastly forward to meet death, often deliberately choose it, even plan it long beforehand. The only light in the darkness is heroism."[3]

Giants and Other Enemies

For Nordic peoples, Niflheim is the cold, dark realm of the dishonored dead. It is filled with clouds, heavy frost, and freezing chasms covered with ice—much like the wild northlands themselves. From this dark and freezing world, the enemies of the gods of Asgard arose—the Frost Maidens and hostile giants. They want not only to destroy the gods but also the sun and the moon, bringing darkness, chaos, and death to the world.

Loki's sinister daughter Hel is the ruler of the dead in Niflheim, where a mighty river, clogged with huge chunks of ice and discarded weapons, separates the land of the dead from Midgard, the land of the living where mortals reside. Hel is often depicted with half of her body white and the other half black. A ferocious four-eyed dog named Garm guards the entrance of her dark realm. This huge hound, his chest drenched with blood, is similar in many ways to the hellhound Cerberus, the watchdog of the underworld in Greek mythology.

Hel rules over oath breakers, evildoers, and those unfortunate people who die from sickness and old age. She is so cruel and coldhearted that she refuses to release the beloved god Balder, even though the creatures of heaven and Earth and the gods of Asgard weep bitterly and beg for his return. None of the Aesir have any authority over her in the world of the dead, so they cannot force her to return handsome Balder to his pleading mother, Frigga. The English word *hell* comes from this giantess who rules the icy underworld.

For the long-ago Norsemen, the world of mortals, or Midgard, was also peopled with cruel and treacherous creatures, such as dwarfs, gnomes, and trolls. Generally, trolls

Fiery Volcanoes

Iceland has 130 volcanoes. In 2010 one of these erupted. The enormous ash plume disrupted air travel across Europe for several weeks. The fiery description of the end of the world in Norse mythology may have been inspired by a similar volcanic eruption in Iceland.

were thought to be evil and dangerous, although sometimes they interacted peacefully with people. They were clever at making things of stone and metal and often lived in caves or among rocks. Early stories describe trolls as giants who live in castles and roam during the night. When exposed to sunlight, trolls turn to stone. The large rocky crags of Troldtindterne (Troll Peaks) in central Norway are said to have once been two armies of trolls that fought a great battle—until sunrise caught them and turned them to stone. Over time, trolls came to be portrayed as about the size of humans or, in some cases, as small as dwarfs.

Dwarfs, who were said to breed like maggots far beneath the earth, were highly skilled metalworkers and artisans with supernatural powers. For a price, they often made special gifts for the gods, such as a magic spear for Odin, a ship for Freya, and a hammer for Thor, the god of thunder. But the dwarfs were unpredictable and spiteful, as were their neighbors, the black elves of the mines, who kept watchful guard over underground stores of gold, copper, and precious gemstones. The Norsemen were afraid of them.

Some writers, like H.A. Gerber in *Myths of the Norsemen*, have ventured a conjecture that the dwarfs so often mentioned in ancient sagas and fairy tales were real beings, probably the Phoenician miners, who, working the coal, iron, copper, gold and tin mines of England, Norway, Sweden, etc. took advantage of the simplicity and credulity of the early inhabitants to make them believe they belonged to a supernatural race and always dwelt underground in a region which was called Svartalfaheim, or home of the black elves.[4]

Always on guard against such evil opponents, Nordic warriors, as well as farmers, kept their swords and battle-axes at hand, prepared for any unexpected encounter with giants, trolls, and dwarfs. Even if a warrior never actually saw one himself, he was convinced that one day he would stand with the gods to fight against such fearsome enemies at the battle of Ragnarok.

Ragnarok—End of the World

Ragnarok, or the doomsday battle of the Norse gods, is unique in all the world's collected mythologies. It foretells of a great battle between good and evil and reveals that the Aesir gods are doomed. Ragnarok describes how they will lose their final battle to the Frost Giants and Mountain Giants, their longtime enemies, who represent all the brutal powers on Earth. The term *ragnarok* means "fate or doom of the gods." It is a complete and terrifying account of the end

The Andreas Stone with a relief of a scene from the Norse poem "Ragnarok," in which the god Odin is eaten by Fenrir the wolf.

of the world. First, there will be three bitter winters with no warm weather in between. Families will take part in bloody feuds and personal conflicts. Good moral behavior will disappear. The mythic wolves Skoll and Hati will devour the sun and the moon, plunging the world into darkness. Even the stars will disappear from the heavens.

Then three golden roosters will crow, signaling to the giants, the gods, and the valiant dead that the end-time has come. Violent earthquakes will shake the foundations of the world. Fenrir, the terrible monster-wolf, will be set free from his bonds. Jormungand, the mighty sea serpent, will churn up tidal waves that carry the evil giants toward the battlefield. The god Heimdall will blow his horn to call Odin and his sons to battle, along with the dead warriors residing in Valhalla.

According to the Norse myths, the noble Aesir and Vanir die, along with the human heroes. Odin is swallowed by the monster-wolf, Fenrir. His son, the mighty Thor, drowns in venom from the Jormungand, or World Serpent, after he slays it. Frey is slaughtered by a giant, and Tyr dies battling Garm, Hel's monstrous hellhound. Heimdall and Loki face each other for the final time. Both die. Then the world is destroyed by a devastating fire. The scorched earth sinks into the sea. The description is a vivid one with fire and smoke rising to the stars and then a tidal wave swallowing the flaming land. According to the tale, which is recorded in the *Poetic Edda*, the god Balder and his wife are reborn to have a family that will start a new race of deities. One human couple, who fell asleep in the mighty branches of Yggdrasil, or the World Tree, survive the devastation and start a new race of humans.

Kings, Warriors, Slaves

The Vikings' worship of their gods also reflected their class structure. Their society could be divided into three basic categories—the jarls, karls, and thralls. The jarls, or earls, were the most powerful members of Norse society. Often they were wealthy chieftains. While kings were chosen from families with royal blood, the provincial governors and rul-

A Viking sells a slave to a Persian merchant. Slave trading was a major source of income for Norsemen.

ers were selected from the jarls. Generally, they claimed Odin, chief of the gods, as their most important deity. They believed Odin and his mighty son Thor could bring them victory or defeat in battle. Neither chieftains nor warriors lived to be old. They did not want to. They feared dying like cattle in the straw. During the peaceful reign of Haakon the Good (935–961), one Viking warrior complained, "I was afraid I might come to die of old age, within doors on a bed."[5] The Vikings preferred to die in battle so they could live in Valhalla with Odin and the gods. There it was always sunny and warm. The singing was lively, and the mead and roasted pork never ran out.

The Nordic people were generally content with their rulers—as long as the crops and animals were plentiful and the women had many healthy babies. But when the weather was bad and the crops failed or disease afflicted both people and animals, the people blamed the king. It was not uncommon for

Captivating!

The English word "enthrall" means to capture the fascination of, or to hold spellbound. It is derived from thrall, the Old Norse word for "slave."

a despised king to be mysteriously strangled in the night. Others were presented as human sacrifices to Odin, when killing a thrall or slave did not bring about the desired results.

The kings soon learned that it was to their advantage to be as much like the gods as possible, so the people would trust them and follow them as leaders. Some of them succeeded. Many of the kings and chieftains were described as larger-than-life heroes with personalities like Thor's. One such king was Olaf, son of Tryggve and great-grandson of Harald of the Fair Hair. Olaf became king of Norway in 995. He is described by history scholar Will Durant as

> a very merry frolicsome man, social and very generous . . . stout and strong, the handsomest of men, excelling in bodily exercises every Northman that ever was heard of. . . . He could run across the oars outside his ship while men were rowing; could juggle three sharp-pointed daggers, could cast two spears at once and cut equally well with either hand.[6]

Most Vikings were karls, or freemen. They were proud and independent. They had the right to bear arms. Many owned their own homes and land. Most were farmers, fishermen, sailors, merchants, and craftsmen such as leather tanners, jewelers, and blacksmiths. But, because only a firstborn son could inherit land or wealth from his father, many karls who were not firstborn sons owned no land at all. Still, many of them became quite wealthy by selling slaves, spices, or imported glass and silk from the Byzantine Empire. Karls generally worshipped Thor and Frey, the god of fertility, and they were the backbone of the Scandinavian invasion forces when it was time to go to war or on raiding expeditions.

Thralls were slaves. They were on the lowest rung of society's ladder. Slave trading was one of the Norsemen's primary sources of income. Often the slaves were foreigners taken from their homelands during Viking raids and brought back to northern Europe. The slaves represented a wide range of ethnic groups, such as Irish, English, French, Spanish, Dutch, and even Iranian. Thralls were given the dirtiest and toughest tasks that the free karls did not want to do for themselves. This included taking care of sheep and pigs, which were considered dirty, lowly animals. The slaves also carried manure to fertilize the fields and chopped piles and piles of firewood. Women slaves performed domestic chores. Thralls were not allowed to own weapons. Their hair was cut short. They were often killed as human sacrifices to the gods.

The Sea Wolves

The Vikings had a mythic love of the sea and were willing to risk treacherous adventures to explore, raid, and trade with people in foreign lands. They believed that the Norns, or Fates, controlled their destinies. If they were destined to return as heroes, they would. If they died at sea, the Fates had determined that it would be so. The sailors and fishermen

For centuries, people from Spain to Russia feared Viking dragon ships because the Vikings were known to plunder villages and to kill or enslave the inhabitants.

Mischief Maker

The Norse gods had to defend themselves and their realm from their sworn enemies, the Frost Giants, and also from a character named Loki, who is sometimes described as a god and sometimes as the offspring of two Frost Giants and not technically a god. Author Kenneth C. Davis describes the complicated relationship Loki had with the Aesir:

The supreme trickster god of uncertain parentage, Loki might be the offspring of the giants—the sworn enemies of the gods. But he is a frequent companion of the gods Odin and Thor. At times destructive and mischievous, Loki is also an appealing god who helps the deities out of difficulties—usually the very ones he has created.

In the Eddas of Snorri Sturluson, Loki is described as "pleasant and handsome in appearance, wicked in character and very changeable in his ways. He had much more than others that kind of intelligence called cunning. . . . He was always

placing the aesir into the most difficult situations; and often extracts them by his wiles."

Kenneth C. Davis. *Don't Know Much About Mythology.* New York: HarperCollins, 2005, pp. 303–304.

The Loki Stone depicts the Norse god of mischief, Loki, known to be wicked in character and a trickster.

looked to Odin to bless their efforts. They also worshipped Njord, the sea god, and prayed that he would bring them good luck. This deity was held in high esteem, and many small coastal towns in Norway were named in his honor.

The Norse built fine wooden ships. Many had fierce dragons or the heads of sea serpents carved on the prow. Their longships were the best oceangoing vessels of their day. They were light, swift, and easy to maneuver. Several well-preserved ships discovered in the nineteenth and twentieth centuries provided historians with proof of the seaworthiness of Norse ships. They also built freighters that were shorter and designed to carry 15 to 20 tons (13.6 to 18.1t) of cargo, including livestock, trade goods, slaves, and other plunder. Sometimes, the seamen took their families with them on trading expeditions.

For hundreds of years, from the eighth to the fifteenth centuries, Europeans from Spain to France and east to Russia lived in fear of sighting the dragon boats on the horizon. Everywhere the Danes, Swedes, and Norwegians raided, they earned the reputation as fierce warriors, pirates, robbers, plunderers, and bloodthirsty villains. The Vikings even dragged their ships across land to get to major rivers, such as the Volga and Dnieper in Russia. Then they spent weeks raiding the towns and villages and monasteries up and down the river. They eventually reached the Caspian Sea and the Black Sea and sailed into Constantinople, the capital of the Byzantine Empire, in 839. (It is now the city of Istanbul in Turkey.) Impressed with their capabilities as warriors, the Byzantine emperors hired them to be personal bodyguards. They were allowed to roam the city streets and bustling bazaars without a military escort. When he was young, Harald Hardrada, who was king of Norway and Denmark from 1047 to 1066, served as the commander of the emperor's personal bodyguard—a force of five hundred Norse warriors.

Hard and wild, the men of the north conquered lands in Russia, Pomerania, Frisia, Normandy, England, Ireland, Iceland, Greenland, Italy, and Sicily. According to historian Will Durant, "These ventures were not invasions by masses of soldiery like the Moslem hijad or the Magyar flood; they were the

Viking Voyage

In 1984 Norwegian Ragnor Thorseth set sail with his family and crew in a replica of a one-thousand-year-old Viking *knar,* or freighter, named the *Saga Siglar.* In good weather, the ship reached 8 knots, or nearly 10 miles per hour (16kph). They completed the round-the-world voyage in two years.

reckless sallies of mere handfuls of men, who thought all weakness criminal and all strength good, who hungered for land, women, wealth, and power and felt a divine right to share in the fruits of the earth."[7]

No one knows why the Vikings first took to the seas to plunder their European neighbors. Some scholars say it was because of overpopulation and poor harvests. The custom of passing on the family farm and wealth to the firstborn son left younger brothers without an inheritance. These men took to the seas in search of fortune and often became much richer than their older brothers. Historians also point out that the Norsemen's love of adventure—and their longing for a heroic death so they might live with Odin in Valhalla— might also have fueled their desire to join a Viking raiding party.

CHAPTER 2

The Heroic Gods of Asgard

Some have said that the myths and sagas of the Norse are as wild and massive as the high wooded mountains of Scandinavia. Many find these myths particularly appealing because of the tales of great adventures shared by the brave gods and goddesses. Like the Olympians in Greek mythology, the Norse gods have human personalities, but they are not as frivolous and they are not invincible. Some of the Norse gods, the Aesir and the Vanir, live in a city of palaces called Asgard. They are constantly on the alert against attacks from their enemies, the Frost Giants, who live in a mountainous city called Jotunheim. The gods of Asgard are often somber and grim because they know that when the end of the world comes, the giants will win the final battle, as described in the doomsday myth of Ragnarok.

Still, the gods face their doom with undaunted courage, always ready to fight another battle with brave determination. The gods of Asgard have the personality traits and physical characteristics that the people of the north admired most. These include courage, physical strength, and wisdom born from hard-earned experience. The goddesses are resourceful, beautiful, and brave—the same traits that the Norse admired in their women.

Odin and His Wife

Odin is the one-eyed ruler of the gods living in Asgard. More quiet and solemn than the Greek god Zeus, Odin is often shown wearing a cloud-gray cloak with a blue hood. He lives in a golden palace called Gladsheim in the city of Asgard. He remains aloof from the other gods and goddesses and rarely eats, even with the heroic slain warriors who come to feast in Valhalla. Instead, he feeds his meal to the two wolves, Geri and Freki, which crouch at his feet. Two ravens, named Hugin (Thought) and Munin (Memory), perch on his shoulders. Each day, Odin sends the ravens into the world to bring him news about what men on the earth are doing. He also has a mighty eight-legged stallion named Sleipnir. When huge black clouds and strong winds would blow across the mountains and plains, the Norsemen declared it was Odin riding a galloping Sleipnir across the stormy sky.

Armed with a mighty spear called Gungnir and donning his eagle-shaped helmet, Odin's responsibility is to keep the Frost Giants at bay, to postpone as long as possible the doomsday battle in store for the gods of Asgard. He even gouges out one of his own eyes to gain more wisdom regarding how to do this. After seeking the Well of Wisdom that is guarded by the giant Mimir the Wise, Odin demands a drink of water from the well. Mimir consents—on the condition that Odin give up one of his all-seeing eyes. Odin agrees, knowing that his newfound knowledge will benefit both the gods and mankind.

In order to learn the secret of the runes, a strange script used in mysterious secret rituals, Odin again has to make a sacrifice. He willingly pierces himself with his own spear. He hangs in agony on the World Tree, called Yggdrasil, for nine days and nights. After this painful ordeal, he possesses full knowledge of the runes, which he shares with humans. The people of the northern nations adapted the runes to their earliest alphabet and used the odd characters for both record keeping and inscriptions.

Frigga is the wife of Odin and queen of the gods. It is said that she can see into the future while sitting next to Odin on his throne, but nothing can entice her to reveal what she knows. Sometimes referred to as the mother god-

dess or earth goddess, Frigga brings fertility to both the land and the people who live upon it. She presides over marriage and childbirth. Pregnant women pray to her while they are in labor so that she will bless them with the safe delivery of their infants. Also known as the goddess of the clouds, Frigga is often depicted wearing snow-white gowns or dark gray garments, depending upon her mood. She is tall, stately, and beautiful, with heron plumes in her hair and a jangling cluster of household keys around her waist—the symbol of a conscientious housewife.

Frigga can also fly, wearing a magical cloak made from hawk and falcon feathers. Some say she is able to shape-shift into a real falcon while flying. When hardworking farmers in the rye and barley fields would hear the screech of a soaring falcon overhead, they would pause to look up, believing that Frigga was checking on the crops. Although she frequently spends time with Odin at Gladsheim, Frigga owns her own

A ninth-century picture stone depicts Odin riding the eight-legged horse Sleipnir. The Norse believed that storms and winds were caused by Odin riding his horse across the sky.

Days of the Week

The days Tuesday, Wednesday, Thursday, and Friday were named for Tyr (Tiu), Odin (Woden), Thor, and Frigga. Tyr was the god of war. Odin was the greatest of the Norse gods. Thor was his son, and Frigga was Odin's wife, the queen of the gods.

palace, called Fenslir, or the Hall of Mists. While there, she spends her time spinning clouds or golden threads upon her jeweled spinning wheel. As the goddess of housewives and motherly love, Frigga invites those husbands and wives who had been kind and faithful to one another in life to dine with her in Fenslir after they die.

Because she is a queen, she has many lovely handmaidens to wait upon her and to run errands for her. One of the most important is Syn (Truth). She guards the doors to Frigga's palace and refuses to let in anyone the goddess does not wish to see. Once Syn shuts the door upon a would-be intruder, she cannot be coaxed to open the door for any reason. Frigga, also recognized as the goddess of justice, would send Syn to preside over trials and tribunals. When a decision would be vetoed or rejected, Syn was declared to be against it, and that decision became final.

The Mighty Thor and Tyr

Thor, the god of thunder and lightning, is the eldest son of Odin and Frigga. In some northern regions, such as Norway, he was the most important deity of all and more popular than his father Odin during the Viking age. The patron god of peasants and the lower classes, Thor is often described as a typical broad-chested Norseman with bristly red hair and beard, and muscular arms and legs. Normally good-tempered, Thor can be provoked into a terrible rage. He is stronger than any human that ever lived, it was said. In all the world, only his father Odin is stronger. Thor owns a magic hammer called Mjolnir, which means "crusher." A blow from Thor's hammer causes instant death. It is like a boomerang that always returns to his hand after he hurls it.

Despite his lethal weapon, Thor was considered a benevolent god. It was believed that he only hurls his lightning bolts at Ice Giants and other enemies. Destructive hailstorms and violent cloudbursts were blamed on the malevolent storm gods, not Thor. His hammer was so sacred to the Norse that a replica was used to drive in boundary stakes, to secure an oath or vow, and to solemnize marriages. Thor never rides on horseback but is often depicted driving a shining, rumbling chariot drawn by two huge goats, with sparks flying from their teeth and hoofs. Thor's beloved wife is named Sif, the Golden-Haired. Her long blonde hair covers her like a veil, trailing out behind her like the tall pale grass in the northern harvest fields.

Tyr, the god of war and courage, is also considered the god of law and order. He is said to be Odin's son by a beautiful but angry giantess who is like the raging sea. Others say

Thor: A God of the People

Thor is often described as the most popular god among Viking warriors. Odin was the most powerful and important, but Thor was someone the Vikings could relate to. Author Kenneth C. Davis explains:

Second in importance in the Norse pantheon after Odin, Thor is ruler of the sky, the god of lightning and thunder.
. . .

Immense in stature, with a great red beard, Thor has flaming eyes and a huge appetite. He is the most popular Viking god, because his life reflects the values of Viking warriors. A generous and gentle giant, he flies into a great rage when provoked.

Kenneth C. Davis. *Don't Know Much About Mythology.* New York: HarperCollins, 2005, p. 305.

Thor, the god of thunder, was second in importance to Odin. This tenth-century figurine, found in Iceland, depicts the god of thunder.

A sixth-century bronze plaque depicts the god Tyr, left, battling the monster Fenrir.

he is the offspring of Odin and Frigga. Although he has no special palace of his own in the city of Asgard, he is always welcome at Valhalla and Odin's palace and is considered one of the twelve most important Aesir deities. Tuesday, the second day of the week, is named in his honor.

Tyr's symbol is the sword, and all those that worshipped him had the sign, or rune, of Tyr's sword engraved upon their own sword blades for good luck. Tyr's own mighty sword was fashioned by the same dwarfs who made Odin's magic spear. The Norns had declared that whoever possessed the sword would always win battles over his enemies. Tyr is often depicted as having only one hand or one arm because he was maimed by the monster-wolf, Fenrir. By the Viking age, which is commonly said to be the eighth through eleventh centuries, Tyr was nearly forgotten as a deity. Viking warriors preferred to worship Thor and Odin. But many place names still exist that give testimony to how important Tyr was considered at one time—the Tyrol region in Austria being one of the most well known.

The God of Wisdom and Poetry

Another son of Odin and Frigga is Bragi, the god of wisdom and poetry. Bragi plays a magical golden harp and sings songs celebrating the heroic adventures of Norse heroes and gods. It is said that his music and poetry make dead trees bloom with new buds and leaves. His heavenly music greets the slain warriors who arrive at Valhalla. Bragi was so venerated, or respected, by the northern tribes that skalds and storytellers were referred to as Braga-men or Braga-women. On special occasions, whether festive or solemn, the Vikings drank a toast to Bragi in cups shaped like a ship. The sacred sign of Thor's hammer was made over the cups, and then the head of the family or the king or chieftain solemnly vowed to perform some great deed of valor within a year's time. Many of his guests also made similar pledges, which they were also obligated to keep within a year's time. It was not uncommon for some men, after drinking too heavily, to make excessive vows that they failed to keep within the year's time. Some scholars say this is how the word *brag* came to be part of our vocabulary.

Bragi is married to Idun, the goddess who keeps golden apples of eternal youth in a special casket and feeds them to the gods so they can live through countless ages. Although her husband Bragi is always depicted as an older man with a long white beard, Idun is young, beautiful, and strong—a symbol of spring and eternal youthfulness.

Attila and Tyr's Sword

According to legend, Attila the Hun discovered a sword buried on a riverbank in A.D. 434. He was convinced that it was the Sword of Tyr. Attila and his barbarian horde became the most feared enemy of the leaders of the Roman Empire and of Gaul, modern-day France.

The Twin Deities

Odin and Frigga also had twin sons named Balder and Hodur. The god of the sun, Balder is also the most beloved of all the gods. He was beautiful and good-humored. Loki, the trickster giant, who was jealous of Balder, fooled Hodur, who was blind and ugly, into killing his brother. All the gods and everything on the earth mourned his death. For centuries, the Norse celebrated the anniversary of Balder's death with a festival on midsummer's eve, or the summer solstice. On that day, the longest of the year, the people built huge bonfires and spent the day outdoors, watching the sun and drinking toasts to Balder the Beautiful and Beloved.

Frey and his sister Freya, also twins, are the god and goddess of fertility. They too are important in the Norse pantheon. They are the children of the sea god, Njord. Frey is said to be handsome and personable. He is associated with warm, sunny days and soft, summer rain showers. He possesses a number of marvelous gifts, given to him by the gods or dwarfs. One of them is a special sword. It has the power to fight and win a battle all on its own, as soon as Frey draws it from its sheath.

Frey also owns a powerful steed called Blodughofi that can run across flooding rivers and dash through blazing fires upon command. He also possesses a magic ship that can change sizes. When necessary, it stretches large enough to hold all the gods and goddesses, their horses, and their battle equipment. When not in use, it can be folded up as neatly and small as a handkerchief and tucked away until Frey needs it again.

But this god's most prized possession is the great, golden-bristled boar named Gullinbursti. It is said that the beast's golden bristles represent sun rays. Others say they are symbolic of the golden grain in the harvest fields. Farmers were particularly grateful to Frey and his magic boar, for not only did they bless the crops, but the animal taught man the art of plowing when it first dug up the earth with its powerful tusks. Many warriors wore boar-head helmets to inspire fear in their enemies. Boar's flesh, or pork, was eaten each year for the annual Yule celebration. The first night of festivities began on the longest night of the year in December. The pig's head would be crowned with laurel and rosemary leaves and carried to the table for all to admire. Although the Yuletide season is now associated with Christmas, it was first celebrated in honor of Thor and Frey.

Blue-eyed and golden-haired Freya is the second most important goddess after Frigga. Like Venus or Aphrodite in the Roman and Greek myths, she is the goddess of love and beauty. It was said that she pays particular attention to the prayers of lovers. She rides across the heavens in a swift chariot drawn by two large cats. Half of all the warriors slain in battle are offered to her in tribute. While Odin's hand-maidens, the Valkyries, carry half of the slain to Valhalla, Freya rides down to the battlefield to claim the remainder for herself. These she carries back to Folkvang, her spacious palace in Asgard.

Freya also welcomed pure maidens and faithful wives to join her in the afterlife. To do so was so enticing that many Nordic women joined their husbands on the battlefield, hoping to be reunited with them in Freya's hall. Other women volunteered to be burned on their husbands' funeral pyres.

Loki tricked Hodur into killing Balder. As depicted here, Balder's corpse is placed on a ship to burn, his wife is also on the funeral pyre, and the giantess Hyrrokkin pushes the boat out to sea.

Blue-eyed and golden-haired Freya, the goddess of love and beauty, rode the battlefields in a chariot drawn by cats and carried the dead to her palace in Asgard.

Other Important Deities

Hermod, another of Odin's courageous sons, is valiant in battle. Sometimes he accompanies the Valkyries on their ride to the earth to help escort slain warriors to Valhalla. Odin even entrusted Hermod with his mighty spear and ordered him to throw it over the heads of the warriors on the battlefield to rekindle their courage during combat. Swift and nimble, Hermod is also the messenger of the gods. Like the Greek god Hermes, Hermod wears a special helmet and carries a magic wand.

Distinguished by golden teeth that flash when he smiles, Heimdall is the god of the dawn. He can see for hundreds of miles on a clear day. Because Heimdall has such keen eyesight, Odin made him the watchman of Asgard. His duty is to guard Bifrost, the rainbow bridge that leads into the divine city. Heimdall's hearing is so sharp that he can hear the grass growing in the fields and the wool growing on the backs of sheep. Armed with a mighty sword, Heimdall wears gleaming white armor and carries a large horn that he was ordered to blow whenever he sees enemies approaching.

Carvings on the ninth-century Gosforth Cross (a detail is shown here) depict several scenes from Norse mythology, including Vidar avenging his father's death by killing Fenrir the wolf.

Frigga's Spinning Wheel

It was said that on clear Scandinavian nights one could see Frigga's spinning wheel or distaff in the stars. The Greeks named this same constellation Orion's Belt, after the mythical hero hunter who was slain by Artemis, goddess of the moon.

Uller is the god of winter. He is usually depicted wearing a heavy cape of fur and magic wooden skis or ice skates made of bone. His mother is Sif, and Thor is his stepfather. He loves the cold weather and excels at archery and hunting. Numerous temples were dedicated to Uller in Norway and Sweden. On the altar lay a sacred ring upon which important oaths were taken. The oath taker placed the ring on his hand before making his pledge. It was said that this ring would shrink quickly, severing the finger of anyone who lied or took an oath falsely.

Vidar is the god of silence and revenge. His father is Odin and his mother is a giantess named Gridr. It is said that he is the second strongest of all the gods. During the battle of Ragnarok, Odin is killed by the wolf Fenrir. Vidar avenges his father's death by killing the monster-wolf with his bare hands. Pressing one mighty foot upon the wolf's lower jaw, Vidar grabs the beast's upper jaw and tears him apart.

Vali is the son of Odin and a giant princess named Rinda. The baby Vali grows with amazing speed, reaching adulthood in a single day. Armed with a bow and arrow, Vali races to Asgard where he kills Hodur, avenging the death of the beloved Balder. Odin grants him one of the twelve seats in his palace and relays the news that Vali is destined to survive the last battle of the gods, along with Vidar. He is described as an accurate marksman with his bow and arrow and regarded as the god of eternal light.

The North and South

There are many similarities between the gods and goddesses of Asgard in northern Europe and those that dwell on Mount Olympus in Greek and Roman mythology. It is easy to observe that beautiful Freya is similar to Venus, or Aphrodite, the goddess of love. Robust Frey is often compared to Apollo, and fearless Tyr to Mars, or Ares, god of war. Others have pointed out that Bragi, the eloquent Norse god with his harp, has much in common with Orpheus, the Greek musician who plays the lyre with such skill that even the birds listen to him sing. Odin, like Zeus, is described as majestic and middle aged. Both had love affairs with attractive females other than their wives and fathered a family of superheroes. For both the Norse and the Greeks, the realm of the dead is guarded by fierce dogs: Garm guards Hel's gates, and three-headed Cerberus protects the entrance of Hades. While singing their cruel song, sirens in Greek mythology lure unsuspecting sailors to their deaths. The northern Lorelei possesses the same evil gift.

Even the creation myths have similarities. H.A. Guerber points out,

> The Northern nations, like the Greek, imagined that the world rose out of chaos; and while the latter described it as a vapory, formless mass, the former, influenced by their immediate surroundings, depicted it as a chaos of fire and ice—a combination which is only too comprehensible to any one who has visited Iceland and see the wild, peculiar contrast between its volcanic soil, spouting geysers, and the great icebergs which hedge it around during the long, dark winter season.[8]

Also interesting is that twelve mighty gods sit in Odin's council hall, while that same number assemble on the peak of Mount Olympus in Greek mythology. But there are differences between the Greek and Norse myths that directly relate to the culture of the north. For instance, while the Greek gods and goddesses dine on nectar and fruity ambrosia, the hearty Norse gods drink mead and eat roasted boar flesh. While the Greeks believed nightmares escape like breezes from the Cave of Somnus, the Norse insisted female dwarfs and trolls carry bad dreams up from deep crevasses of the earth at night and use them to torment humans. Both the people of the cold north and those of the warmer climates in Greece and Italy chose to represent the earth as a mother figure. But the Greek goddess Demeter (and her Roman counterpart Ceres) is depicted as friendly and generous. On the other hand, Frigga of the north is often cold, mysterious, and unyielding.

In the Greek myths, the god Vulcan and the one-eyed Cyclops produce all the magical weapons used by heroes in the stories. In the tales of the Norsemen, the dwarfs manufacture magic swords, necklaces, and unbreakable chains. While the Greek deities are depicted wearing light tunics of linen with sandals on their feet, the Norse gods dress in heavy, layered clothing with capes and cloaks made of fur or feathers. They usually wear armor as well. Always on the alert for attacks by the Frost Giants, the Aesir need to be battle-ready.

CHAPTER 3

Tales of the Sword and Axe

N ot surprisingly, a culture in which the cruel rites of human sacrifice were common would have tales of violence, swords, and battle axes. Even humorous tales, such as the theft of Thor's hammer, end in blood shed. One of the main themes in Norse mythology is the importance of courage in the face of overwhelming odds and ultimate doom. Any hero who could exhibit bravery in grim circumstances was considered worthy of lasting fame, even after death. While the Greek and Roman gods are often considered to be friendlier and more companionable, the myths of northern Europe reflect a harsher universe populated by fierce giants and monsters that are a continual threat to both the gods and mortals. Popular Greek mythology is often praised for its rich and lyrical language and for its fantastic creatures, such as the winged horse Pegasus. The stories of Norse mythology have not been as popular. However, in her book *Scandinavian Mythology*, H.R. Ellis Davidson states, "The stories of their gods and giants and legendary heroes deserve to be more widely known. Their strength and imaginative power, humor, clear-sightedness and somber magnificence surely merit a place for them beside the myths of ancient Greece and Rome."[9]

In the Norse creation myth, the universe is held in place by the giant tree Yggdrasil. The roots of the tree extended from Asgard to Niflheim.

BAXTERS Patent Oil Printing 11 Northampton Square

Norse Creation Myths

According to the earliest recorded Norse myths, the creation of the world took place when two regions—fiercely hot Muspel and ice-cold Niflheim—merged together. At that moment, a Frost Giant named Ymir is born. A primeval cow named Audhumla is also created. Her milk gives Ymir the nourishment he needs to live and grow. In time Ymir gives birth to three offspring from the sweat of his armpits and leg—two males and a female.

The cow Audhumla receives nutrition from an enormous salt block. As she licks it, a large handsome man emerges from the block of icy salt. His name is Buri. In time, his son Bor marries a Frost Giantess named Bestla. They have three sons named Odin, Ve, and Vili.

But Ymir is brutal, and when Odin and his brothers have grown to maturity, they slaughter the giant. The heavy blood flow drowns all the Frost Giants except two—Bergelmir and his wife, who escape in a boat crafted from a hollowed tree trunk. Bergelmir vows to take revenge on Odin and his brothers—a vow that his descendents also take seriously. This explains the constant warring between the gods of Asgard and the angry Frost Giants.

After killing Ymir, Odin and his brothers use the dead giant's body parts to make the earth. Using his shattered teeth and bones, they make the rocks and stones. From his ribs they form the mountains. From his blood they form the lakes and rivers. Ymir's skull becomes the sky. The sparks from the fiery southern region of Muspel are used to create the stars, the sun, and the moon. And from Ymir's brain they form the clouds in the sky.

When Odin sees two logs lying on the beach, he turns them into the first humans, a man and a woman named Ask and Embla. According to the Norse creation myth, all humans descended from these two people. This land that lies between Muspel and Niflheim Odin names Middle Earth, or Midgard. Everything is supported or held in place by a colossal sacred tree called Yggdrasil. The roots of the tree stretch into Asgard, the heavenly dwelling place of Odin and the other gods. The roots also grow down into Niflheim's icy world and also to Jotunheim, the city of the giants. The Norns live at the base of the huge tree, controlling the past, present, and future of all men and women on the earth. A rainbow bridge called Bifrost connects Asgard, where the gods dwell, with Midgard, the dwelling place of humans. From his lofty throne in Asgard, Odin keeps watch over the entire world.

Norse men, women, and children never tired of hearing the same tales of their gods repeated over and over again. Battle-scarred Viking warriors enjoyed songs and riddles as well. They sat around the fires at night listening to

A Bucket of Apples

In 1903 a Norwegian farmer discovered an oak Viking ship buried on his property. Known as the Oseberg ship burial, the grave contained the corpses of two well-dressed women and a wealth of burial goods—including a bucket of apples, the symbol of fertility and eternal youth.

the skalds tell the familiar tales of their favorite Norse heroes and gods. The poets sometimes made up new stories about local chieftains and kings. If these stories pleased the rulers, the skalds were handsomely rewarded with gold or jewelry. Sometimes the skalds were killed because they unintentionally offended a bad-tempered leader. Davidson states, "The gods of the North, whose roots like those of their own World Tree go down into the darkness of the past, are deities to command our respect and stir our imagination."[10]

Tyr and the Mighty Fenrir

In most Norse myths, the hero's victory is usually earned at a high cost. Tyr, the god of war and courage, is often depicted missing his right hand. He did not lose it on the battlefield as one might suppose: It was bitten off by Fenrir the wolf, one of Loki's monstrous offspring. Fenrir, like his hideous sister Hel and his serpent-brother Jormungander, were kept hidden by their father in a deep cave. But Fenrir and his monstrous siblings kept growing and growing, until Odin took notice of them. Fearing the combined strength of the monsters, Odin tossed Hel into Niflheim to rule over the nine gloomy worlds of the dead. He flung the gigantic serpent into the deepest northern sea. Odin then took Fenrir with him back to Asgard, hoping to tame the beast as he had done with his own pet wolves Geri and Freki.

But Fenrir would not be tamed. He grows larger and fiercer with each passing day. The gods, fearful for their lives, try twice to bind the monster with huge chains. Fenrir breaks his bonds each time. Finally, the gods petition the dwarfs to manufacture a magical chain that would restrain the beast forever. With their magical arts, the dwarfs make a chain so slender that it resembles a strand of silken flax. Fenrir, suspicious of the strange-looking chain, refuses to let the gods bind him with it—unless one of them agrees to place his or her hand between his massive jaws while the binding takes place.

The gods hesitate. Then courageous Tyr steps up and thrusts his right hand into the wolf's mouth. The other gods bind the beast with the magic chain. Fenrir struggles and

An eighteenth-century Icelandic manuscript depicts the wolf Fenrir biting off the hand of the god Tyr. Fenrir would be chained up in Asgurd only to be magically released in the final battle of Ragnarok to slay and devour Odin.

tries to free himself. But no matter how he twists and strains, he cannot break loose this time.

As the gods cheer, Fenrir bites off Tyr's hand. From that day on, the fearless god of war wields his sword with his left hand and carries his shield on the stub of his right arm. Some scholars suggest that this myth explains why Tyr is also considered the god of law and order, with Fenrir representing the control of violent crime. In the final battle of Ragnarok, Fenrir is freed from his magical restraints. He kills Odin and then devours him. Vidar, one of Odin's sons, avenges his father's death by slaying the wolf-monster.

Thor and the Colossal Serpent

Victory and death often go hand in hand in the myths of the Norsemen. This can be seen in the stories about Thor and Jormungander, the World Serpent. This monster was the serpent-dragon offspring of Loki, the god of evil. After Odin flung the enormous creature into the depths of the ocean, it continued to grow until its mighty coils could circle the entire earth. The beast's mighty jaws could clutch its tail in its mouth like an enormous ouroboros, or serpent swallowing its tail. When it rolled and writhed in the depths of its watery domain, the serpent generated huge, lashing waves. Thor is said to have encountered the dragon-headed beast on numerous occasions—once while fishing with the giant Hymir.

This eighteenth-century Icelandic manuscript depicts Thor capturing the serpent Jormungander on a fishing expedition. Thor would later use his hammer to kill the monster.

Using the head of a cow for bait, Thor casts his line. Immediately, Jormungander chomps down upon the head, swallows it, and plunges back down beneath the thrashing waves. Thor tugs on the line, using all his mighty strength to snag the beast. The struggle goes on for hours. Finally, the tension of the fishing line seems to slacken, and Thor realizes that the dragon-serpent is weakening. With a mighty jerk, he pulls the repulsive creature halfway out of the waves and prepares to kill it with his famous hammer. Hymir, however, is so terrified by the dreadful beast that he quickly cuts the fishing line with his sword. The colossal serpent sinks down into the depths of the sea.

Thor does not see the great beast again until Ragnarok—the day of the last battle, when each god must battle a ferocious monster to the death. On that fearful day, Jormungander flings itself upon the shore and uncoils its loathsome body. Thor stomps down to the beach to face it. The earth trembles violently as the two opponents meet in mortal combat. Thor hurls scorching lightning bolts, and the serpent writhes and heaves. Finally, Thor brings his mighty hammer down on the serpent's dragonhead. The beast roars in pain before it collapses lifelessly upon the shore. Moments later, Thor dies too, a victim of the poisonous venom that gushes from the creature's open mouth.

The Theft of Thor's Hammer

Not all of the myths are about battles and beasts, however. Some of the stories reflect the Vikings' lively sense of humor, such as the tale of the theft of Thor's hammer, the mighty god's most prized possession. When he awakens one morning and discovers that it is gone, Thor is angry. He is a little fearful too. If the Frost Giants learn that the hammer is missing, they might storm the gates of Asgard and destroy the gods.

Thor's angry cries of dismay attract Loki's attention. When Thor explains that his prized hammer is missing, Loki begins snooping around. He soon discovers that

The Swastika

The swastika, or hooked cross, is associated with the worship of Odin. This ancient symbol has been found on sword hilts and scabbards in Denmark and Anglo-Saxon England. It was believed to bring victory in battle. German Nazis adopted the symbol as their own in the twentieth century.

The Beginning and the End of the Universe

The Norse creation myth not only explains how the universe, the earth, the gods, and humans were created, it also describes the end of the world in the doomsday battle called Ragnarok.

The wolf Hati will finally catch and swallow the sun, and the wolf Skoll will finally catch and swallow the moon. The giant Surt will tear apart the heavens with his scorching flames. . . . The earth will shake so forcefully that the trees of the forests will become uprooted and the mountains will collapse. . . .

Odin will fight against Fenrir; Thor will pit himself against the world Serpent; and Frey will battle Surt. The wolf will swallow Odin whole, but Odin's son Vidar, the fiercest of warriors, will tear Fenrir's jaws apart and kill him. Thor will slay the serpent, but its poison will kill him. Heimdall and Loki will kill each other and Surt will slay Frey. Thus the high ones will be destroyed. . . .

With the fire from his flaming sword, Surt will set the entire earth ablaze. People will flee their homesteads in fear. With death as their destiny, the doomed and trembling human race will walk the road to join Hel. Finally, the charred and devastated earth will sink into the sea.

Donna Rosenberg. *World Mythology: An Anthology of the Great Myths and Epics.* Chicago: NTC, 1994, pp. 212–213.

Thrym, a Frost Giant prince and a destructive thunder deity, has stolen Thor's magical hammer and buried it deep underground. When confronted by Loki, Thrym refuses to give it back unless Freya, the goddess of beauty, agrees to be his bride. When Loki delivers this message to the Aesir, Thor is indignant. Freya is outraged. She refuses to agree to the marriage. The other gods and goddesses point out how defenseless they are without Thor's mighty weapon, but Freya still refuses.

Then Heimdall, the lookout guard, proposes a plot. He suggests that Thor dress in a wedding gown and veil and pretend to be Freya. Thor, eager to retrieve his hammer, agrees. The giant Thrym is delighted to welcome his lovely bride-to-be and prepares a wedding feast in her honor. During the banquet, Thor consumes an ox, eight large salmon, cakes, and other sweets. He washes it all down with two barrels of mead. Thrym is a bit surprised by the bride's enormous appetite, and he cannot help noticing the blazing eyes that flash at him dangerously through the filmy wedding veil.

After the meal, the giant calls for Thor's sacred hammer to finalize the marriage. The mighty hammer is laid in the bride's lap, as is customary at weddings. Thor seizes it by the short handle and instantly kills Thrym and all the invited guests. Then he flings aside the dress and veil and returns in triumph to Asgard, where he is greeted by the hearty applause of the relieved gods.

Idun's Apples of Immortality

Idun is the personification of spring and eternal youth. When the young wife of Bragi arrived with a magic casket filled with the golden apples of eternal youth, she was warmly welcomed by the residents of Asgard. She willingly shared this fruit with the gods, who were not immortal. They were eager to eat the fruit, which helped to preserve their beauty, strength, and vitality.

But Idun did not share the fruit with dwarfs and giants or humans. One day, the ancient storm giant Thiassi, disguised as an eagle, swoops down and kidnaps Loki. Gripping the trickster with his deadly talons, Thiassi threatens to kill Loki if he does not help him to lure young Idun out of the heavenly city so that Thiassi can obtain some of the magic apples to eat.

Loki agrees. As soon as he is released, Loki makes his way to the groves of Brunnaker where he finds Idun passing the time of day. He tells the young goddess that he has discovered a tree with apples just like her own magical ones. Idun does not believe him. Loki insists that she come with him to see. He also suggests that she bring a crystal bowl with some of her own fruit, so they can make a comparison. As soon as the two of them cross the boundary of the heavenly city, Loki abandons her. Thiassi, who has been watching and waiting, swoops down and carries Idun away. But Thiassi cannot convince the captive Idun to give him a taste of her magical apples. She grows more pale and sad with each passing day. She sighs. She weeps for her husband Bragi and her friends in Asgard. But no matter how he rages and rants, Thiassi cannot scare her into sharing the fruit with him.

Idun, the goddess of spring and eternal youth, shared her apples with the gods to preserve their strength, beauty, and vitality.

Months and months pass, and soon the gods and goddesses feel their own youth and beauty diminishing. They are dismayed to discover that Idun has been kidnapped. All-knowing Odin goes to Loki for an explanation. He threatens to kill him if the young goddess is not promptly returned. Borrowing Freya's falcon wings, Loki flies off to Thrymheim, where Idun is being held hostage. He finds her there alone and crying. Some accounts say that Loki turns the young goddess

into a small bird. Others say he turns her into a nut and flies off with her in the direction of Asgard, where the gods and goddesses stand watch, eagerly awaiting her return. They had even built a massive bonfire to light the way home for her.

Thiassi soon discovers that his captive is missing. Donning his eagle plumage, he flies after Loki and Idun. But he is old and not as strong as he had been. As he approaches the watchtowers of Asgard, he is overcome by the heat and smoke from the bonfire. Thiassi collapses, and the gods slay him without mercy. Afterward, they welcome Idun back home and feast together on the magic apples, which restore their vigor and beauty. Like the Greek myth about Persephone, who is whisked away to the underworld by the god Hades, the tale of Idun and the magic apples was the Norse way of explaining the change of seasons: warm spring and summer when Idun is safe at Asgard and cold, desolate fall and winter for the months she was kidnapped and away. For the long-ago Nordic people, apples were a symbol of fertility, abundance, and good health.

The Death of Balder

The sun god Balder was the most beloved of all the Norse deities—even among the gods. To prevent his injury and death, his mother Frigga demanded that all creatures on the earth swear an oath not to harm her precious son. The goddess made even the natural elements, such as fire, wind, and ice, take the same oath. Balder's invincibility fascinated the other gods. They often amused themselves by throwing boulders, weapons, and other objects at him. The young god would laugh good-naturedly. No matter how accurately they aimed or how large the object, nothing could harm him.

But the trickster Loki was jealous of Balder's good looks and popularity. Disguising himself as an old woman, he visits Frigga one day as she sits spinning in her palace. Loki asks in a thin, crackling voice if it is true that everything on the earth had sworn an oath not to injure young Balder. Frigga admits that it is so. She had received the promise from everything on the earth—everything except the small mistletoe plant that grows in the branches of the mighty oak tree outside the

An eighteenth-century illustration depicts the malicious Loki manipulating Hodur into killing Balder.

gates of Valhalla. It was so small and harmless, Frigga had not thought it necessary to ask it to swear an oath.

Armed with this information, Loki hobbles away to search for the mistletoe plant. He finds it growing in the huge oak tree just as Frigga had told him. He casts a spell upon the small plant, making it stronger and larger than it normally would be. Then he crafts an arrow from one of the twigs. He patiently waits until the Asgard gods resume their game with Balder. Noting that Hodur, Balder's blind twin, was not participating, Loki offers him a bow and the mistletoe arrow. He offers to guide Hodur's aim.

Eager to take part in the fun, Hodur accepts. As he fires the arrow, he waits to hear the roar of laughter. Instead, he hears a groan of pain as Balder, fatally wounded, collapses. This is followed by horrified cries from the other gods. Balder's wife Nanna takes one look at the lifeless body of her husband and drops dead with grief beside him. Distraught,

both Frigga and Hodur order courageous Hermod to go to the realm of
the dead and beg Hel to release Balder.
Hermod bravely makes the dangerous
journey and is heartened when Hel tells
him that she would release Balder on
the condition that all things living and
nonliving shed a tear for the dead sun
god. As the entire world is mourning
Balder's death, Hermod is certain that
he can win the young god's release.

The gods and goddesses of Asgard
journey from one end of the world to
the other, ordering all things on the earth to weep for Balder.
Even the rocks and mountains weep. But the coldhearted
giantess Thok, hiding in her cave, refuses to shed a tear for
Balder. And so Hel will not release him. Discovering that Loki
is responsible for the tragedy, the gods seize the trickster and
bind him tightly in a deep, dark cave. They tie a venomous
serpent over his head. As the venom drips from the beast's
open mouth onto Loki's face, it causes him unbearable agony.
Sigyn, his wife, tries catching the venom in a cup, hoping
to ease his pain. But when the cup is full and she leaves his
side to empty it, the dripping venom falls on his ravaged face
once more.

Whenever there was an earthquake, the Vikings would
nod and shrug and declare that it was only Loki convulsing
with pain.

Food for Strong Stomachs

Lutefisk is a popular dish in Nordic
countries. It is cod soaked with
poisonous lye until it has a gelatin-like
consistency. It is served baked or boiled.
Hakarl is fermented shark meat left to
rot in the ground for six weeks, then cut
in strips and served on a toothpick.

Sigurd the Dragon Slayer

Not all of the popular Norse tales are about gods and goddesses. Sigurd is the greatest human hero in Norse mythology. More than half of the *Poetic Edda* is dedicated to his
exploits.

The son of a murdered king, Sigurd owns a magical horse
named Grani, the offspring of Odin's own steed Sleipnir. He
also owns a marvelous sword called Gram. It was crafted
by a dwarf named Regin from the broken bits of Sigurd's

A tenth-century woodcut depicts Sigurd killing the dwarf Regin as part of a plan to take possession of Fafnir's treasure and golden ring.

father's sword. It is so powerful that it can cut through an iron anvil. Using Gram, Sigurd avenges his father's death by slaying King Lunge, his father's killer. Sigurd also slays the king's men and achieves great fame as a mighty warrior.

After this, Sigurd kills a powerful dragon named Fafnir. He first digs a pit near the riverbank close to the dragon's lair and hides in it. When Fafnir leaves his legendary treasure cave to drink from the river, he passes over Sigurd's hiding place. The hero thrusts his sword into the dragon's heart and stabs the beast to death. After licking the dragon's blood, Sigurd discovers that he has the gift of understanding the language of birds. From the birds, Sigurd learns that the dwarf Regin intends to kill him and claim the dragon's treasure for himself. So Sigurd slays Regin first and takes

First Man and Woman

In the Norse creation story, the first man was named Ask, and the first woman was named Embla. Below is the method of their creation as told by Snorri Sturluson in his Prose Edda.

When they were going along the sea shore, the sons of Bor [Odin, Ve, and Vili] found two trees and they picked these up and created men from them. The first [son of Bor] gave them spirit and life; the second, the understanding and power of movement; the third, form, speech, hearing and sight. They gave them clothes and names. The man was called Ask and the woman Embla; and from them have sprung the races of men who were given Midgard to live in.

Snorri Sturluson. *The Prose Edda: Tales from Norse Mythology,* trans. Jean I. Young. Berkeley: University of California Press, 1954, p. 37.

The first man and woman, Ask (right) and Embla, were created from two tree trunks by Odin and his brothers Ve and Vili.

possession of the treasure, including a powerful gold ring.

Sigurd later rescues a beautiful Valkyrie named Brynhild. Because she had disobeyed Odin, the mighty female warrior is put into a deep sleep as punishment, and her bed is surrounded by a flaming wall of fire. Only the bravest warrior who knows no fear can rescue her. Sigurd does so, and the two fall in love. He gives her the magic gold ring, unaware that the ring is cursed and all who own it soon die. Later, Sigurd is bewitched into marrying a woman named Gudrun. He loses all memory of Brynhild and their love for one another. When Sigurd is slaughtered in his sleep by another warrior, Brynhild is heartbroken. Unwilling to live without him, she asks to be allowed to burn with him on his funeral pyre. Then she kills herself.

The prose *Saga of the Volsungs*, written in Iceland in the 1100s, tells the stories more fully. The tales about Sigurd later inspired those written about an imaginary German hero named Siegfried in the *Nibelungenlied*, or "Song of the Nibelung," a famous German epic poem written in the 1200s. German composer Richard Wagner used the tales as the basis for his famous series of operas, *The Ring of the Nibelung*.

CHAPTER 4

Hanged Men and Dragon Ships

For the Norsemen, the myths were more than just a collection of heroic tales. They impacted their daily lives at every level. The stories encouraged social customs and behavior and religious practices. For example, when the people saw two ravens circling above them in the sky, they knew that Odin's birds, Hugin and Munin, were watching them. At night, when they heard the howl of a wolf, they shuddered and wondered if the monster-wolf Fenrir was roaming the northern wilderness. As farmers harvested their crops, they remembered to leave grain in the fields for Sleipnir, Odin's eight-legged stallion.

Brides wore red at their wedding because it was Thor's favorite color. Betrothal rings, too, were usually set with a red stone, such as a ruby or garnet. Artisans preserved the tales of writhing serpents and fire-breathing dragons in their gold, silver, bronze, and pewter art objects. Craftsmen carved birds and battles on the smooth surfaces of reindeer antlers and walrus tusks. Warriors wanted to achieve glory at any cost, so they might die and live again to fight alongside Odin, Thor, and the other gods of Asgard at the great battle of Ragnarok. Kenneth C. Davis, the *New York Times* best-selling nonfiction author, has described the Vikings as "a gang of lawless bikers—bad to the bone—until they finally settled down

Discovered in a burial mound in 1904, the Oseberg ship was part of a Viking grave thought to be that of a queen and contained treasures, artifacts, and supplies for the journey to the afterlife.

and became the respectable civilized Scandinavians they are today. But was it all pillage, rape and destruction or was there a kinder, gentler Viking? The answer is—not really."[11]

Sickly babies or malformed infants were left outside on the mountainside or on the beach to die or be eaten by predators. Society had no place for boys not strong enough to fight or girls not healthy enough to breed strong sons. Those children who were allowed to live were raised to honor the gods and work hard. They participated in vigorous leisure activities too, such as swordplay, swimming, ice-skating, and archery, which prepared youngsters to be strong in battle when they grew up. Board games such as *hnefatafl*, in which one player must protect a king from the pieces of another

player, prepared boys and young men to think strategically—an important skill for a successful warrior. Women often fought beside their husbands, brothers, and sons in the hope that the goddess Freya would see their courage and take them to live in Folkvang, the palace where faithful wives and pure maidens could enjoy eternal life. Nor was it uncommon for women or girls to volunteer to die upon the funeral pyres of a great chieftain, so that they might serve him in the afterlife at Valhalla.

Just as the Norse honored the brave and beautiful goddesses of Asgard, such as Frigga and Freya, they also honored their queens with earthly tributes and lavish funerals. Some highborn women were even given magnificent ship burials. This consisted of placing the corpse in a wooden ship, along with the dead person's worldly possessions. The funeral ship was then buried. A series of women's ship graves was uncovered at Tuna in Vastmanland, Sweden. They contained many treasures, including beautiful gold jewelry and silk ribbons. Perhaps the most famous ship grave was discovered in Oseberg, Norway, in 1904. It is the richest Viking grave ever found. It contained the skeletons of two women. They are thought to be the remains of an elderly queen and her younger handmaiden, who was probably strangled so that she could serve her mistress in the afterlife. The exquisite oak ship contained an elaborately carved four-wheel cart, four sledges for pulling supplies, horse gear, textiles, supply chests, a tent, beds, and other household supplies.

The Temple at Uppsala

Worshipping Odin and Thor was of utmost importance to the individual and the community. Odin was so important to the people of the north that both royal family members and chieftains attempted to trace their genealogies to him. One of the most sacred sites in northern Europe was at Uppsala in Sweden. Here, at the temple of Odin, men and horses were

Saving the Best for Sacrifice

The Nordic people were not the only ones who sacrificed horses. In ancient Rome, a special chariot race was held each October on the Field of Mars. The right-hand horse on the winning team was then sacrificed to the god Mars to ensure good crops the following year.

sacrificed to honor the god. Most of the victims were captives of war. They were strangled, then stabbed with a spear, and their corpses were hanged from a tree in the sacred grove that surrounded the temple. Historians speculate that during ancient times, Scandinavian kings may have been killed in the same manner every nine years. James George Frazer, a renowned expert in the study of myth and religion, relates the story of King Aun of Sweden who sacrificed nine of his own sons to Odin. With each sacrifice the king lived nine more years, seemingly as a blessing from the gods, who were pleased by the sacrifice. Frazer writes that Aun, who was quite old and frail, "would have sacrificed the tenth and last, but the Swedes would not allow him. So he died and was buried in a mound at Uppsala."[12]

Long after Christianity was introduced to the region, Odin worshippers still made the required sacrifices to appease him. The eleventh-century German clergyman and historian Adam of Bremen visited Uppsala. He reported seeing the bodies of both men and horses hanging from the trees in the sacred grove near the temple. He noted that a special festival was held at nine-year intervals and that everyone from all of Sweden's provinces was expected to attend. "Of every living thing that is male, they offer nine heads, with the blood of which it is customary to placate gods of this sort. The bodies they hang in the sacred grove that adjoins the temple. Now this grove is so sacred in the eyes of the [Vikings] that each and every tree in it is believed divine because of the death or purification of the victims. Even dogs and horses hang there with men."[13]

Such ceremonies were considered essential for a prosperous life and to please the gods. These rituals were so important that when Haakon the Good, king of Norway from 935–961, refused to participate, the people were angry and fearful. They were certain he had offended Odin and that the entire countryside would be punished. Haakon was Norway's first Christian king. When he ascended the throne, the annual feast of bloodletting took place as usual. That the new king participate in the ritual was considered important. According to custom, a horse was butchered and boiled in a large cauldron. Haakon was presented with a cup of the hot, bloody broth to drink and a slice of horseflesh to eat to start the festivities. As a Christian, he refused to participate in the pagan ritual. He merely opened his mouth over the plate of steaming meat. This angered many of his subjects. Others feared that Odin would punish them for the king's disrespect.

Holy Horseflesh

The ritual of sacrificing horses was also important in the rituals of Norse religion, particularly in the worship of Frey. The god of fertility and agriculture was considered the third most important god after Odin and Thor. In Iceland, if an owner dedicated a stallion to the god Frey, it was forbidden for anyone—on pain of death—to ride the sacred horse before it was sacrificed to the god. The horses were slaughtered at temples dedicated to Frey. Two of the most important were located in Trondheim in Norway.

Also dedicated to Frey, the temple area at Thvera in Iceland was so sacred that it was said no criminals dared to go near it for fear of being punished by the god. Sometimes oaths were sealed there. A gold ring would be dipped in the blood of the sacrificed animal, and those taking the oath would promise to keep their word, swearing by the names of Frey, his father Njord, and the almighty Odin.

Because Frey was the god of farming and fertility, horse fights were a popular rite of spring. It was believed that such fighting between fierce stallions ensured good crops. The fights have been depicted on memorial stones and mentioned in the sagas. The victorious horse was later sacrificed to Frey. The feet and skull were preserved, and the horse-flesh cooked and eaten in a ceremonial meal. Horses were so important in the worship of Frey that remains of dead horses have been found inside and around the Viking ship burials in Norway, Sweden, and Denmark. It was believed that burying horses with the deceased would ensure fertility in the next life. In Iceland horses were found in two such ship burials of men believed to have been priests of Frey.

Other animals considered worthy enough to be sacrificed to the gods included white or black bulls and male sheep and goats. The boar was particularly prized as a suitable offering to Frey and the other Vanir. Only healthy, perfect animals could be offered as a sacrifice. In honor of Frey, wild boar was eaten at the annual Yule feast in December. The animal's head would be decorated with laurel and rosemary and carried into the banquet hall for all to see. According to H.A. Guerber, the father or head of the household would lay his hand on the platter and acknowledge "the boar of atonement, swearing he would be faithful to his family and would fulfill

Honoring the Boar

Because it was a ferocious, cunning beast, the wild boar was highly esteemed by early Nordic people. The animal's razor-sharp tusks could seriously injure men, dogs, and horses. A boar's head was frequently used as an ornament on the helmets of northern kings and warriors, whose bravery was unquestioned.

Shown here is a bronze statuette of the Swedish god of farming and fertility, Frey.

his obligations, an example that was followed by all present from the highest to the lowest. This dish would be carved by a man of unblemished reputation and tried courage, for the boar's head was a sacred emblem which was supposed to inspire everyone with fear."[14]

Legal Eagles

It may seem ironic that law and order was considered extremely important to a people known as sea raiders and pirates of the northern seas. Odin and Thor were recognized as the major gods of law and order. Tyr was also considered an upholder of justice. Despite the acceptance of a monarchy and a ruling class, the people of the north had a surprisingly law-abiding society. Landowners acted as legislators and judges at the local *hus-thing* or assembly. Slaves and women were not allowed to speak at the assemblies. There was also a provincial assembly known as the *Thing* and a national *Althing*. Laws and public judgments were passed at these assemblies. Before the laws were written down, individuals known as lawmen were required to memorize large portions of the laws and rules established by the assembly. They served as advisers and consultants to those with a case to plead or defend. In Iceland these individuals were known as the lawspeakers. Chieftains were also required to memorize large portions of the established law and to use their power and influence to enforce the law.

Most of the Nordic laws related to civil disputes. The Norse were proud and independent, but they were quarrel-

The Vikings were surprisingly democratic. Landowners acted as legislators and judges at assemblies called Things *or* Althings.

some, too. Family feuds were long-lived and bloody. In her book *A History of the Vikings,* author Gwen Jones mentions the strict regulations about "boundary marks, hunting rights, flotsam and jetsam, the felling of trees and collection of firewood, infringements of grazing and the like; to libel, satire, calumny, the making of love songs, sheep-stealing, turning people's butter sour and wooing their bees."[15] There were also laws against murder, manslaughter, and disrespect of holy places dedicated to the gods. Penalties for breaking the law were often harsh and carried out promptly while the assembly was in session. One who killed his mother or father was hung by the heels from a tree next to a live wolf that was similarly hung. Rebels against the government were dragged to death behind a wild bull. Arsonists were burned at the stake.

In Iceland the law assembly met once a year on a large flat plain called Thingvellir. The meeting was officially called to order in the summer on a Thursday—the day dedicated to Thor. It generally lasted for two weeks and coincided with the annual feast to honor Balder. Like the other legal assemblies throughout Scandinavia at the time, the purpose of the annual gathering was to make new laws, discuss old ones, and to settle disputes. Interestingly, much of the European sea laws in force today are based on ancient Norse laws. Some of the earliest Norse laws were written on parchment and still exist. These written records provide details about rules regarding legal weights and measurements and the policies concerning the ruling of port cities and commercial markets.

Legal Language

The term *Danelaw* was once used in the British Isles to identify those regions where Vikings lived and ruled. Over time, Scandinavian vocabulary words such as law, bylaw, and outlaw became accepted as English words too.

Nordic Navigators

With the best oceangoing vessels of their day, the seafarers of northern Europe were the first to visit four of the world's continents. They had keen navigational skills. They knew where they were going and how to get back. They knew that the earth was round. They seldom navigated using the stars, as did other early seafarers. Instead, they used the sun. Based on archaeological evidence, some scholars believe the Norsemen used a sailing instrument known as a bearing dial or sun compass. This helped them judge the angle of the sun. The dial is a wooden half-disk marked at thirty-two equal intervals with a pin in the middle of the disk. This device could be used to read the angle of the sun and get one's bearings at sea. It is believed that the early Nordic sailors also had simple tide tables and navigational calculations based on the angle of the sun at different times of the year.

Many brave and adventurous Nordic men and women took to the seas looking for a better future. Some sailed west to Iceland and Greenland. Seafarers from Norway colonized these islands. The settlement in Greenland provided trade goods greatly valued by European kings and other wealthy customers. These included furs, walrus ivory, falcons, polar bears cubs, and narwhal horns. Some historians believe that the spiraling horn of the narwhal gave rise to the medieval myths about unicorns. From Greenland, Nordic seamen sailed across the Atlantic Ocean to North America, nearly five hundred years before Christopher Columbus was given credit for discovering the New World.

The Vikings even started at least one colony in Canada. Archaelogists have confirmed that an ancient site discovered at L'Anse aux Meadows, located at the northern tip of Newfoundland, is Norse and not, as originally believed, a Native American camp. Discovered in 1960, the site contains the remains of turf houses similar to those so common in Scandinavia at the time. There was also evidence of ironworking and a smithy, Nordic tools, and even a bronze cloak pin. Scholars estimate that the settlement was established in the year A.D. 1000, which coincides with the saga of Leif Eriksson's voyage to Vinland.

Based on their own written records, Nordic mariners were bold and confident. They knew their ships were well built. They dedicated their voyages to Odin and trusted him to guide the way.

Norse Pioneers and Christian Authority

Guoriour Porbjarnardottir was one of the pioneers of the Norse colony in Canada. In the mid eleventh century, she made a pilgrimage to Rome. Some believe she spoke with church authorities about the settlement, because a Catholic bishop was later appointed to Greenland, and his jurisdiction included unnamed regions west of the island.

The Norse seamen's voyages to North America may possibly have inspired Christopher Columbus. In his autobiography *Historie di Cristofor Colombo*, which was published by his son after the explorer's death, Columbus claims to have traveled to Iceland in February 1477. Local legend claims that Columbus actually spent the winter on a farm on the Snaefellnes peninsula, in the western region of the island, after arriving on a Lisbon merchant vessel that had come to trade Mediterranean goods for dried fish. Some historians speculate that Columbus gathered valuable information there about the New World.

In fact, in 1476 a Norwegian seaman named John Skolp showed a Portuguese expedition a sea-lane that led across the Atlantic Ocean, past Greenland, and straight to the Labrador coast. The Norsemen were using this route routinely before Columbus's famous 1492 voyage. In his book *The Norsemen*, German historian Eric Oxenstierna considers

Viking navigators founded a settlement at L'Anse aux Meadows in Newfoundland, Canada, nearly five hundred years before Columbus discovered America.

Viking Artifact in Maine

The Maine Penny is the only confirmed item of Viking origin that has been found in the United States. The tiny Norwegian coin was discovered by archaeologists near the mouth of Penobscot Bay in Maine in 1957. It was minted by King Olaf Kyrre between A.D. 1067 and 1093.

reasons why Columbus did not follow the familiar northern sea lanes: "So why didn't Columbus undertake his long voyage in the Santa Maria westward via Greenland to Labrador, which would have been shorter, less dangerous, and far more conclusive? Not for a moment did Columbus doubt their existence . . . the ice cold waters of the north did not interest him. All he wanted was to find an easy sea route to India. That was the only undertaking for which he could raise either interest or money."[16]

Twilight of the Gods

As the Danes, Norse, and Swedes raided other parts of Europe, they were introduced to Christianity. They often noticed that life was easier and the lifestyles richer in these Christian countries. They began to suspect that perhaps other gods were more powerful than Odin, Thor, and Frey. Some Norsemen converted to Christiantity while overseas and took their faith back to their homeland when they returned. The new faith had practical attractions for Viking rulers. It was civilized and scholarly, with well-enforced laws and teachings such as the one about the divine right of kings. This medieval political and religious doctrine supported the idea that kings derived their right to rule from God, so they could not be opposed by their subjects or institutions such as the Church. Christian countries also had more political status than pagan nations. By becoming Christians, the Vikings were welcome to trade with and travel to other Christian countries. However, many Viking chieftains and kings were reluctant to give up the old gods. Although he was a pagan, King Horik II of Denmark sent presents to the pope in Rome in 864. But like other Viking rulers, he was reluctant to convert to Christianity.

In the summer of A.D. 1000, the Icelandic chieftains met as usual for the *Althing* and discussed whether the island should remain loyal to the gods of Asgard or embrace

Christianity. There were fervent followers in both camps. The problem was brought before Thorgeir Ljósvetningagodi, the law-sayer, or lawspeaker. Although he was a pagan, both sides agreed to abide by his decision. Thorgeir retired to his tent to think about his decision. He remained there all day and all night. The next morning at the Law Mound he announced that Icelanders should convert to Christianity. Anyone caught sacrificing horses, eating horseflesh, or performing other pagan practices would be outlawed for three years. Following the announcement, Thorgeir tossed idols of Odin and the other pagan gods into the Godafoss waterfall. Because of his decision, Iceland became the first official Christian country in Scandinavia.

Battle scene from the reign of King Olaf Haraldsson. When Haraldsson destroyed the pagans' statue of Thor, rats and snakes spilled from it, causing the horrified pagans to convert to Christianity.

Olaf Haraldsson, King of Norway from 1015 until 1028, also tried to convert his people to Christianity without bloodshed. Militant pagans at Gulbrandsdal in central Norway resisted. When Olaf journeyed to the region to fine them for their offense, they met him near a huge wooden idol of Thor, which they had worshipped for years with offerings of gold jewelry and food. Olaf ordered one of his warriors to club the idol. When the rotten wood shattered, rats the size of cats tumbled out of the statue, along with snakes and other vermin. The pagans were horrified. Olaf suggested that the gold rings and bracelets would look better on their wives and daughters than on the remains of the shattered idol. Challenged to fight for their wooden god or accept Christianity, the residents readily agreed to convert.

Gradually, life in the north began to change. Many admired the story of Jesus, who reminded them in some ways of their beloved Balder. Over the centuries, the Norse gave up the old gods and embraced the new religion. However, they maintained familiar Viking imagery by placing dragon heads on the roofs of their stave churches and incorporating the shape of Thor's hammer into the Christian cross.

CHAPTER 5

New Life for Ancient Gods

In a world where storytelling has a universal appeal, it is little wonder that Norse mythology has been embraced by people in other cultures. Both children and adults, once exposed to the tales of Nordic gods and heroes like Sigurd, find the stories of rugged nobility and daring adventure appealing. Because these stories stir a deeper feeling and understanding in the reader, the heroic myths of the Norsemen have grown in popularity in literature, art, music, and film around the world. The centuries-old tales have influenced pop culture and world history. The ancient gods of Asgard have also found new life in role-playing games and Japanese animation. The Norse gods are regularly featured in the American TV series *Stargate SG-1*. In New Zealand, a new television comedy-drama called *The Almighty Johnsons* borrows heavily from Norse mythology. The main character Axl Johnson is Odin reincarnated. Axl's brothers are also reincarnated Norse deities—Bragi, Uller, and Hodur. They live in present-day New Zealand. But the gods have not quite recovered the full powers from their former glory days in Asgard, and a band of evil Norse goddesses intends to see that they do not.

Norse gods and goddesses, such as Njord and his wife Skadi, appear today on Norwegian postage stamps. And

Viking reenactors participate in games at a festival in Iceland. Viking festivals are popular around the world, including the United States.

while one would certainly expect many places in northern Europe to be named after the Norse gods, in Canada communities such as Baldur, Manitoba, are also named after the gods. A store in Pennsylvania is named Uller's Ski and Snowboard Shop. Many people enjoy ham during the Christmas holidays, a tradition that echoes the popularity of eating wild boar during the Yule season in December in the Nordic countries. Viking festivals are held around the world and in many cities in the United States. Those attending can buy graphic novels featuring tales of the gods and goddesses of Asgard and T-shirts sporting images of Valkyries. Tourists visiting Storsjon Lake in Sweden can take a lake monster cruise in

search of the beast called Storsie. Sightings go back to the early 1800s. The trap used to attempt the beast's capture in the nineteenth century is on display in the local museum. In Norway, Lake Mjosa is famous for its monster sightings that date back to 1522. Visitors can take a boat across nearby Lake Seljord, famous for its elusive sea serpent, not unlike the one killed by Thor—so they say.

In Modern Literature

Many of the heroes, monsters, and gods of Asgard have been reborn in modern literature. Henry Rider Haggard was a popular nineteenth-century British adventure novelist. At the age of thirty-four, Haggard was already a household name. His books *King Solomon's Mines* and *She* are still read today. The adventures of his most popular character, Allan Quatermain, became a model for the Indiana Jones films. In 1891 Haggard turned to the mystical fury of the Vikings in his novel *The Saga of Eric Brighteyes*. Inspired by the Icelandic sagas, Haggard weaves the tale of Eric Thorgrimursson and his love for Gudruda the Fair. But her father refuses to allow Eric to marry his daughter, and Swanhild, the evil sorceress, intends to win Eric for herself. Intrigue, treachery, and battles soon follow. Haggard dedicated this Viking romance to Victoria, Empress Frederick of Germany, the eldest child of Queen Victoria of England. The tale of Eric Brighteyes was so well written that British professor and author J.R.R. Tolkien occasionally referred to it during his college lectures and recommended that his students read it.

Tolkien also captures the dark mood and stark beauty of the Norse tales in his classic *The Hobbit* and *Lord of the Rings* trilogy. Place names like Middle-earth and Myrkwood are taken right from the Icelandic sagas. Some characters' names, such as Gandalf, are also borrowed from the tales of Norse heroes, as are the dwarfs, giants, and elves that come to life in Tolkien's novels. As a child, Tolkien had read the

Vikings in *How to Train Your Dragon*

The children's movie *How to Train Your Dragon* is based on a book by British author Cressida Cowell. It takes place in a fictional Viking world and is part of a nine-book series. Jonsi, a singer from Iceland, wrote and performed the song "Sticks and Stones" for the film.

J.R.R. Tolkien, pictured, author of the popular The Hobbit *and the epic* The Lord of the Rings *trilogy, based the books in part on Norse myths and Icelandic sagas.*

tales of Sigurd the Volsung who slew the dragon Fafnir. He fell under the spell of Norse mythology at that time and taught himself to read the ancient Norse language while still a schoolboy. At the age of eighteen, Tolkien began writing romantic Norse poetry about dragon slayers and elf maidens.

In 1926, while a professor of Germanic and Norse literature at Oxford, he formed a group called the Coalbiters and led them in the reading and translation of the sagas and *Eddas*. Members included several other writers and scholars like C.S. Lewis, George Gordon, Hugo Dyson, and

Neville Coghill. The term "coalbiter" is from the Icelandic *kolbiter*, a teasing term for those people who lounge so close to a burning fire they could easily bite the coals. The members did indeed linger around a fire once a week to talk about the gods of Asgard and the Frost Giants. One evening after a Coalbiter meeting, Lewis invited Tolkien to his apartment to continue the chat about the Aesir. Tolkien stayed longer than Lewis thought he would, but Lewis later wrote to a friend, "Who could turn him out, for the fire was bright and the talk good."[17]

World's Loudest Band Has Viking Flair

Manowar, an American band with Viking machismo, was named the world's loudest band in the *Guinness World Book of Records* in 1984. They have a devoted fan base, particularly in Europe. Their *Sons of Odin* album was released in 2006 and *Gods of War* in 2007.

Lewis and Tolkien soon became close friends. Their literary discussions renewed Lewis's childhood love of Norse mythology. As a boy, one of his favorite books had been *Tales of the Norsemen* by H.A. Guerber. In 1914 at the age of sixteen, Lewis wrote *Loki Bound*, an opera libretto based on Norse mythology. He wanted his school chum Arthur Greeves to set it to music. Years later, after joining the Coalbiters and the writers group known as the Inklings, Lewis began writing the *Chronicles of Narnia* for children. *The Lion, the Witch, and the Wardrobe* was published in 1950. Lewis's publisher feared it would not sell and that the fantasy might even damage Lewis's reputation as a writer of serious adult fiction. Even the critics gave the book bad reviews. They disapproved of the Pevensie children interacting with mythological creatures, such as the dwarfs and giants of the Norse myths and centaurs and dryads from the Greek. However, the book was a commercial success and so were the other six titles in the series. Lewis continued to turn to the Norse myths for inspiration for his tales, transforming Eustace Scrubb into a treasure-hoarding dragon that is later saved by Aslan the Lion, and portraying the wicked Green Witch in *The Silver Chair* as a glistening serpent-monster.

Musical Themes

Norse mythology is a recurring theme in heavy metal music lyrics too. There is even a subcategory of metal music called

Singers perform Richard Wagner's Götterdämmerung (Twilight of the Gods), *the last of Wagner's four operas based on Norse mythology that comprise his epic* Ring of the Nibelung *cycle.*

Viking metal. As the name suggests, the lyrics often focus on the Viking age, the Norse myths, and Nordic paganism. The music is characterized by galloping riffs and atmospheric keyboards. Nordic folk instruments such as fiddles, flutes, and horns are also used. The genre originated with the 1990 album *Hammerheart* by Bathory, a Swedish heavy metal band. They followed their success with two other Viking metal albums, *Twilight of the Gods* in 1991 and *Blood on Ice*. Other notable bands in this category include Enslaved, Moonsorrow, and Falkenbach.

By far, the best-known musician inspired by the myths of northern Europe was German composer Richard Wagner. Beginning in 1853, he composed a series of four operas that comprise *The Ring of the Nibelung*. The story is about a race

of dwarfs and a hoard of gold hidden in the Rhine River, guarded by three Rhine Maidens. The gold is magic. Anyone willing to give up love to craft a ring from the gold will gain wealth and power in the world. Separately, the operas are *The Rhine Gold*, *The Valkyries*, *Siegfried*, and *The Twilight of the Gods*. The cast of characters include many familiar to readers of Norse mythology, such as Wotan (Odin), the dragon Fafnir, and beautiful Brünnhilde. "The Ride of the Valkyries" and the "Magic Fire" are two of the most recognizable songs. The entire *Ring* cycle was performed together for the first time in 1876 in Bayreuth, Germany. They have been popular with opera fans ever since. According to Kenneth C. Davis,

> [Nazi Germany's leader Adolf] Hitler was deeply taken by Wagner's operas, which drew vividly on the world of Germanic heroic myths, pagan gods and heroes, demons and dragons. Hitler understood the deep emotional power of the symbols of these myths. Massive statues of ancient Germanic gods played a prominent role in the Nazi mass rallies at Nuremberg in the 1930s. Hitler grasped the visceral power, as well as the propaganda value, of a shared Teutonic myth in uniting the German people in a master race ideology.[18]

A Nazi Obsession

Heinrich Himmler also was enthralled by the Old Norse sagas and myths. During World War II, Himmler was one of the most powerful men in Nazi Germany. He served as the head of the Gestapo and the *Schutzstaffel*, or SS. He reported directly to Hitler. One of the chief architects of the Holocaust, Himmler believed the ancient Norse deities like Thor, Loki, and Frey had been real people, the ancient ancestors of pure-blooded Germans. He was convinced that ancient Nordic runes contained long lost secrets about powerful weapons and potent herbal medicines. Himmler funded many research expeditions to prove his unfounded theories. He sent historians to the remote hills of Bohuslan in southwestern Sweden to study the tens of thousands of ancient runic carvings there, convinced that these were the sacred texts

A Viking Castle in California

Vikingsholm Castle is located in Lake Tahoe, California. It was built in 1929 by a Swedish architect for Lora Knight, a wealthy Illinois woman. Knight wanted a summer home that reminded her of her vacation in Scandinavia. The castle is now open for tours.

of the ancient Norse race. In 1938 he funded a research expedition to Tibet so scholars could look for traces of the Nordic culture there. In 1939 an expedition was sent to Bolivia to the old Andean capital of Tiwanaku, believed by the Nazis to have been founded by Nordic colonists more than a million years ago.

He believed that the legendary Atlantis had been located in the North Atlantic and founded by the ancient Norse. Many other German extremists followed Himmler's lead. A Munich, Germany, newspaper editor named Rudolf John Gorsleben believed that the *Eddas* held clues to the origins of the so-called Aryan race, Hitler's supposed master race. He wrote editorials encouraging Germans to return to the Old Norse religion. According to Gorsleben, "Aryan men and women had once possessed superhuman abilities and these were revealed in the Edda. He also believed that the Aryan race could regain its purported supremacy on the world stage if it could somehow activate those latent powers once again. In 1925 he founded a study group, The Edda Society, to examine this matter. He described the Eddas as the richest source of Aryan intellectual history."[19]

Himmler took Gorsleben's theories seriously. He often dined with members of the Edda Society, convinced that the Aesir gods, such as Odin, Thor, and Loki, were "beings of pure undiluted Nordic essence, the earliest Aryans. As such, they were the possessors of superior knowledge."[20] Those university professors who did not accept this position were replaced by more cooperative teachers, such as Peter Paulsen. A member of the SS, Paulsen was also a professor of archaeology at the University of Berlin. He was a dedicated Nazi and an expert with a worldwide reputation on the early Vikings. He held a mystical view of archaeology and was fond of the Icelandic sagas and Norse myths. He even named his children Sigurd, Astrid, and Hetha after Norse heroes and heroines. By placing SS officers like Paulsen in academic positions, Himmler planned to control everything that was taught in the German universities.

Viking Mythology in Art

Norse legends and myths have inspired many Scandinavian artists throughout history. The Swedish sculptor Bengt Erland Fogelberg captured the barbaric majesty of Odin, Thor, and Balder in his impressive marble statues of the gods in the mid-1800s. Much of Fogelberg's work is on display at the National Museum in Stockholm, Sweden. Peter Nicolai Arbo was a celebrated nineteenth-century Norwegian painter who specialized in dramatic images from Norwegian history and Norse mythology. Two of his most famous paintings are *Valkyrie*, a warrior maiden with flowing hair, and *Asgardsrein*, which depicts a stormy battle scene in the

Norwegian artist Peter Nicolai Arbo's 1865 work Valkyrie. *Known as the maidens of Odin, Valkyrie led slain warriors to Valhalla.*

sky with the gods of Asgard thundering through the dark clouds. During the 1940s Danish artist and illustrator Oscar Knudsen produced a series of romantic paintings of Norse myths, including *Gathering of the Slain*, *Torment of Loki*, and *Freya*, riding across the sky in her chariot. Knudsen died in 1971, but many of his most popular paintings are now available as posters.

The tales of the Aesir also inspired other artists around the world. British artist Frank Bernard Dicksee made his fortune painting portraits of fashionable English society ladies, but he was also noted for his romantic portrayal of legendary story themes. *The Funeral of a Viking*, which he painted in 1893, is darker and more dramatic. It is a vivid scene of Viking warriors pushing a burning funeral ship off the shore into a stormy sea. Bathory, a Swedish Viking metal band, used the image for the cover of their 1990 album *Hammerheart*.

Early twentieth-century British painter Dorothy Hardy, known mainly for her colorful depictions of hunting hounds and horses, also painted dramatic scenes from Norse mythology, such as *The Binding of Fenris* (Fenrir), *Heimdall*, and *The Death of Balder*. Known as an historical genre painter, J.C. Dollman exhibited his dramatic paintings of *Sif and Thor*, *A Viking Foray*, and *Frigg* (Frigga) *Spinning the Clouds* at the Royal Academy in London from 1870 to 1912. Contemporary American artists like Howard David Johnson also find inspiration from the myths of northern Europe. Using oils, mixed media, and even digital art, Johnson has brought *Odin*, *Fafnir the Dragon*, *Siegfried and Brunhilde*, and other Norse legends to life on canvas.

Throughout the years, Valkyries have been particularly popular with artists, illustrators, and sculptors. Sometimes they are portrayed in a soft, dreamy way, as in *The Valkyerie's Vigil* by Pre-Raphaelite British painter Edward Robert Hughes. Other times,

American Gods, Featuring Norse Gods

The tenth-anniversary edition of fantasy author Neil Gaiman's award-winning novel *American Gods* was released in 2011. Many of the characters are modern personifications of ancient Norse gods, including Balder, Odin, and Loki. The book is currently being adapted for an upcoming HBO television series.

they are shown as hearty, armor-clad warrior maidens with dead men slung over their saddles, as in *The Chosen Slain* by German artist Konrad Dielitz. In 1910 the well-known Norwegian artist Stephan Sinding sculpted a bronze statue of a warrior maiden racing on horseback. It can be seen in Churchill Park in Copenhagen, Denmark. Henry De Groux's *Ride of the Valkyries* is on display at the Royal Museum in Brussels, Belgium. The painting is a more frenzied depiction of battlefield horrors.

Comics and Film

The gods and goddesses of Asgard have enjoyed a long career as Marvel Comics superheroes and villains. Thor, the god of thunder, has been one of the company's longest-running superheroes. The character Thor Odinson made his first appearance in comic books in 1962 in *Journey into Mystery*. He is noted for his superhuman strength, speed, durability, and longevity—thanks to the magic apples of Idun. With his trusty hammer Mjolnir, he has the power of flight, energy absorption, weather manipulation, and dimensional transportation. Other Asgardians such as Odin, Tyr, Vidar, and Heimdall have starred in their own comics, too. Balder the Brave appeared in Marvel's alternate universe as one of the many heroes called upon to deal with the zombie plague in Marvel Zombies. Balder is also one of the many collectible lead figurines available from Classic Marvel Figurines—along with Loki and Valkyrie. Thor's golden-haired wife, Sif, is transformed into a superhuman brunette in the comics. She is portrayed as a mighty warrior woman, matched only by Brünnhilde, the Valkyrie. When Sif is kidnapped by a cruel giant and delivered to Hel in the underworld, Thor rescues her. The two fight numerous villains side by side in numerous comic tales, along with Balder the Brave.

The movie *Thor*, based on the exploits of the comic book god, was released in 2011. It was directed by actor Kenneth Branaugh, who portrayed Gilderoy Lockhart in the 2002 movie *Harry Potter and the Chamber of Secrets*. Chris Hemsworth stars as the thunder god and Sir Anthony Hopkins

From movies such as Thor, *to video games, comics, and television shows, the gods and heroes of Norse mythology live on.*

as his father Odin. Actress Rene Russo plays Frigga, Thor's mother. When Thor is banished to Earth for his arrogance, he lands in modern-day New Mexico, where he is befriended by an astrophysicist named Jane Foster. While fighting to reclaim his lost powers and his mighty hammer, Thor also tries to prevent evil Loki from killing Odin and taking over Asgard. Hemsworth, who received a 2011 Teen Choice Awards nomination for his role in the action film, is scheduled to appear in the upcoming sequel *Thor 2.*

In 2011 another action adventure movie with a Norse mythology tie-in was released. In *Captain America*, Nazi villains invade a Viking castle in Norway in 1942 during World War II. They find a magical source of power, said to have belonged to Odin, hidden in a large wooden door decorated with a carving depicting Yggdrasil, the World Tree. After taking possession of the magic cube, the evil Johann Schmidt, head of the German science division known as HYDRA, hatches a plot he dubs Project Valkyrie to take over the world. The hero Steve Rogers, portrayed by actor Chris Evans, must prevent that from happening. Like Thor, Captain America was originally a Marvel Comics character. Both characters will appear with Iron Man and other Marvel Comics heroes in the upcoming film *The Avengers*, which is scheduled to be released in 2012.

Gaming with the Gods

Norse mythology has long been a popular scenario for both computer and video games. At MythicWars.com, players can enjoy free online browser-based computer games inspired by ancient mythologies. *Norron* is set in war-ravaged Midgard with ten thousand weapons, twenty-thousand pieces of armor, and one hundred quests to choose from. Players select one of fifteen Norse gods for their city to worship and one of four heroes to lead the city to victory. Potential role-playing game participants can even take the *Norron Quick Start Tour* to check out the game plan before actually signing up and logging in.

Odin Sphere by Atlus for the PlayStation 2 is a role-playing game with hand-drawn colorful art and fully voiced dialogue. It was released in 2007. The story is told in five chapters from the perspective of different characters, such as a Valkyrie, a fairy, and a knight. Each protagonist is connected to the royalty of each of the five warring nations in the imaginary world of Erion. The warrior nation of Ragnanival is ruled by the demon Lord Odin and his army of raging Valkyries. Odin invades the fairy forest realm of Elfaria and her fairy subjects. Like the other main characters, Odin wields a weapon, called a Psyper, with a large

The Influence of Sigurd

The heroic tale of Sigurd the Volsung, Norse mythology's greatest human hero, has inspired several well-known modern works of literature and art. Author Donna Rosenberg describes the enduring appeal and influence of this tale:

The tale of Sigurd is an outstanding adventure story containing magic, monsters, love, treachery, and death. The work continues to influence and entertain.

Sigurd is an outstanding adventure story. It contains magic, a monster, cursed treasure, passionate love, violent hatred, jealousy, treachery, danger, and death. Within its pages are both an early version of the Sleeping Beauty and a major source for the tale of the cursed ring that J.R.R. Tolkien used in the *Lord of the Rings* trilogy and Richard Wagner used in his cycle of four operas, *The Ring of the Nibelung*.

Donna Rosenber. *World Mythology: An Anthology of the Great Myths and Epics.* Chicago: NTC, 1994, p. 226.

crystal capable of absorbing energy sparks, called Phozons, which are released when an enemy is slain. The five stories overlap as each country battles over control of a legendary magical cauldron. There is even a volcanic kingdom known as Volkenon, which is ruled by Inferno King Onyx. Game reviewers have praised *Odin Sphere* for its beautiful 2D graphics, unique combat system, and detailed story line.

Dawn of Mana by Square Enix for the Sony PlayStation 2 borrows the myth of Yggdrasil, the giant World Tree, and renames it Mana in this attractive and colorful action adventure game. The tree has eight spirit children who embody the elemental powers of fire, wind, and ice. Released in the United States in 2007, it is a prequel to the game *Secret of Mana*. Those wanting more intense action can try the video action game *Thor: God of Thunder*, based on the popular motion picture. Players will assume the role of Thor, wielding the famous hammer Mjolnir as he tries to save Asgard from legions of monsters, Frost Giants, and trolls. Players earn valor runes to attain new powers, abilities, and upgraded weapons.

Perhaps the stories of the Norsemen do more than reflect a culture's spiritual foundations and provide entertaining explanations of the origins of the universe and natural phenomena. Over the years, scholars have debated many different views of the role that mythology has played in the human experience. Anthropologists and psychologists suggest that myths reach some deep level of human thought, and in the words of poet T.S. Eliot, myths "have roots that clutch."[21] One thing is certain: The ancient tales of the Norse have influenced social customs, language, literature, and law in many countries around the world. The heroes of Asgard have perhaps survived Ragnarok after all.

Introduction: Land of the Far North

1. Donna Rosenberg. *World Mythology: An Anthology of the Great Myths and Epics*. Chicago: Passport, 1987, p. xv.

Chapter 1: A Cold, Harsh World

2. Edith Hamilton. *Mythology: Timeless Tales of Gods and Heroes*. New York: New American Library, 1969, p. 300.
3. Hamilton. *Mythology*, p. 302.
4. H.A. Guerber. *Myths of the Norsemen*. London: Abela, 2010, p. 395.
5. Quoted in Will Durant. *The Age of Faith: The Story of Civilization*. New York: Simon & Schuster, 1950, p. 503.
6. Durant. *The Age of Faith*, p. 503.
7. Durant. *The Age of Faith*, p. 510.

Chapter 2: The Heroic Gods of Asgard

8. Guerber. *Myths of the Norsemen*, p. 569.

Chapter 3: Tales of the Sword and Axe

9. H.R. Ellis Davidson. *Scandinavian Mythology*. London: Hamlyn, 1969, p. 12.
10. Davidson. *Scandinavian Mythology*, p. 19.

Chapter 4: Hanged Men and Dragon Ships

11. Kenneth C. Davis. *Don't Know Much About Mythology*. New York: Harper Collins, 2005, p. 296.
12. James George Frazer. *The Golden Bough*. New York: Simon & Schuster, 1996, p. 324.
13. Quoted in Howard La Fay. *The Vikings*. Washington, DC: National Geographic Society, 1972, p. 19.
14. Guerber. *Myths of the Norsemen*, p. 200.
15. Gwen Jones. *A History of the Vikings*. Oxford: Oxford University Press, 1973, pp. 346–347.
16. Eric Oxenstierna. *The Norsemen*, trans. Catherine Hutter. Greenwich, CT: New York Graphic Society, 1965, p. 263.

Chapter 5: New Life for Ancient Gods

17. Quoted in George Sayer. *Jack: C.S. Lewis and His Times*. San Francisco: Harper and Row, 1988, p. 150.
18. Davis. *Don't Know Much About Mythology*, p. 8.
19. Quoted in Heather Pringle. *The Master Plan*. New York: Hyperion, 2006, p. 79.
20. Quoted in Pringle. *The Master Plan*, p. 196.
21. Quoted in Davis. *Don't Know Much About Mythology*, p. 17.

GLOSSARY

anvil: A heavy steel or iron block with a flat top on which metal can be hammered and shaped.

arsonist: A criminal who deliberately sets fires to destroy property.

artisans: Skilled manual worker or craftsman.

Asgard: Home of the Norse gods.

aurora borealis: The northern lights.

Bifrost: The rainbow bridge that connects Asgard, the realm of the gods, to Midgard, the realm of humans.

boomerang: A curved, flat, wooden missile that returns to the person who throws it.

courtier: A person who attends a royal court as a companion or adviser to the king or queen.

deity: A divine being; a god.

fatalism: The belief that all events are predetermined and therefore inevitable.

fjords: A long, narrow sea inlet between steep cliffs.

mead: A kind of wine made from fermented honey.

mortals: Human beings subject to death.

ouroboros: An ancient symbol depicting a serpent or dragon eating its own tail.

pantheon: All the gods of a certain people, group, or religion.

prow: The portion of a ship's bow above the water.

Ragnorak: Doomsday battle of the gods.

Valhalla: The hall where Odin gathered the souls of warriors who had died in battle.

vermin: Insects and wild animals such as rats; thought to be harmful to crops.

Yggdrasil: A giant tree, known as the World Tree, that links heaven, the earth, and the underworld.

Books

Anthony Mercatante. *The Facts On File Encyclopedia of World Mythology and Legend.* New York: Facts On File, 1988. This hefty volume alphabetizes the major and minor deities in all the mythologies from around the world and includes many fables, fairy tales, legends, and folktales as well.

Karl Shuker. *Dragons.* New York: Simon & Schuster, 1995. A beautifully illustrated collection of dragon tales from around the world, including "Sigurd the Dragonslayer" and "Thor and the World Serpent."

Philip Steele. *Step into the Viking World.* London: Lorenz, 1998. A full-color volume that provides insight into the harsh but fascinating world of the Vikings. Includes instructions with photos for making a Viking war helmet, shield, coiled bracelet, and rune stones.

Ornolfur Thorsson, ed. *The Sagas of the Icelanders.* New York: Viking, 1997. Heroic tales about flesh-and-blood Norsemen and their struggles with travel and exile, crime and punishment, and fate and freedom.

Diane Wilson. *Raven Speak.* New York: Simon & Schuster, 2011. A historical novel for readers twelve years old and up. Asa Coppermane, the daughter of a Viking chief, loves her horse and does not want to sacrifice it for the sake of the clan. The story deals with the harsh realities of cold winters, starvation, and sickness in the ancient world of the Norse people.

Anna Yates. *The Viking Discovery of America.* Reykjavik: The Iceland Review, 1993. A brief book that highlights the story of Leif Eriksson's voyages to North America and the archaeological proof of the Vikings' visits to the New World.

Periodicals

Christianity Today. "Christian History: A Severe Salvation," vol. 18, no. 3, 1999. The entire issue is dedicated to the Christian conversion of the Nordic countries. Well illustrated with lively historic narrative.

Sven Rosen. "The Dragons of Sweden." *Fate,* vol. 4, no. 35, April 1982, pp. 36–45. An interesting historic overview of lake monster and sea serpent sightings.

Videos

"Beowulf." Clash of the Gods, season 1, episode 8. A&E Television Networks for the History Channel. Runtime 45 minutes. Original airdate September 28, 2009. The story of the Viking world's most famous warrior. Could this mythological warrior have been real? Unearthed burial mounds and ancient carvings suggest that Beowulf could have been more than a legend.

"Thor." Clash of the Gods, season 1, episode 9. A&E Television Networks for the History Channel. Runtime 45 minutes. Original airdate October 12, 2009. Was the rise and fall of Thor the Thunder God ancient code for something greater than a legend? The program examines new discoveries that may unlock the truth behind the Thor myths.

Websites

The Encyclopedia Mythica (www.pantheon.org/areas/mythology/europe/norse/articles.html). This site offers the collective myths of Sweden, Denmark, Norway, and Iceland and the shaping of Norse mythology in Germanic Europe. There are 147 articles to choose from.

Norse-Mythology.com (http://norse-mythology.com/The_Nine_Worlds.html). This well-illustrated site provides basic information about the Norse gods and goddesses, along with a glossary of terms and Viking-age quizzes.

The Vikings (www.kidspast.com/world-history/0204-vikings.php). A colorful world history site for kids, with quizzes, quotes, and maps, sponsored by the Kids Know It Network.

INDEX

Fenrir (mythological wolf), 20, 44–45, *45*, 57
Fenslir (Hall of Mists), 30
Films, Norse mythology in, 81–83
Fogelberg, Bengt Erland, 79
Folkvang (palace), 35, 59
Frazer, James George, 60
Frey (deity), 9, 22, 34, 61–62, *63*
    in battle of Ragnarok, 20
    sacrifices to, 62–63
Freya (deity), 9, 34, 35, *36*
Frigga (deity), 9, 39, 40, 51–52
    Odin and, 28–30
    spinning wheel of, 38
Frost Giants, 9, 14, 24, 27, 40
The Funeral of a Viking (Dicksee), 80

G

Gaiman, Neil, 80
Garm (mythical dog), 17, 38
Giants, 9, 17
    genealogy of, *5*
    Ragnarok and, 19, 20
Gods of War (album), 75
Gods/goddesses, Norse
    categories of, 12–13
    genealogy of, *5*
    Greek/Roman deities *vs.*, 27, 38–40, 41
    human characteristics of, 12, 27
Gordon, George, 74
Gorsleben, Rudolf John, 78
Gosforth Cross, *37*
Götterdämmerung (*Twilight of the Gods,* Wagner), *76*
Gram (sword), 53–54
Gridr (giantess), 38
Guerber, H.A., 39, 62–63
Gullinbursti (mythical boar), 34

H

Haakon the Good (king of Norway), 21, 61
Haggard, Henry Rider, 73
Hakarl (shark meat), 53
Hamilton, Edith, 14, 17
Hammer, of Thor. *See* Mjolnir
Hammerheart (album), 76

Harald the Fair Hair, 22
Haraldsson, Olaf (Norse king), 70
    battle scene from reign of, *69*
Hardrada (king of Norway and Denmark), 25
Hati (wolf), 20, 48
Heimdall (deity), 36–37, 48, 49
    in battle of Ragnarok, 20
Hel (giant), 9, 17
Hemsworth, Chris, 81, 82
Hermod (deity), 9, 36, 53
Heroism, 14, 17
Himmler, Heinrich, 77–78
Historie di Cristofor Colombo (Columbus), 67
A History of the Vikings (Jones), 65
The Hobbit (Tolkien), 73, 74
Hodur (deity), 34, 35, 38, 71
    killing of Balder by, *52*, 52–53
Horik II (king of Denmark), 68
How to Train Your Dragon (film), 73
Hrolf (Viking chieftain), 12
Humans
    first, 55, *55*
    origins of, 42–43
    relationship between gods and, 12
    sacrifice of, 22

I

Iceland
    Christianity embraced in, 68–69
    Columbus travels to, 67
    law assembly in, 65
    temple area at Thvera, 62
    volcanos of, 18
Idun (deity), 33, 49–51, *50*

J

Jarls (earls), 20–21
Jormungander (serpent), 20, 46, *46*
Jotunheim (city of giants), 27
Journey into Mystery (comic book), 81
Justice, Nordic system of, 11, 63–65

K

Karls (freeman), 22
King Solomon's Mines (Haggard), 73

PICTURE CREDITS

Cover: Gian Salero/Shutterstock.com
© Anders Blomqvist/Getty Images, 60
© Arctic Images/Alamy, 72
© Bettmann/Corbis, 69
© Chris Hellier/Alamy, 23
© Classic Image/Alamy, 50
© Collection Dagli Orti/Historiska Muséet Stockholm/The Art Archive/ Art Resource, NY, 29
© DEA/G. Dagli Orti/De Agostini/ Getty Images, 63
© Dorling Kindersley/Getty Images, 55
© Gale/Cengage Learning, 4, 5, 6
© Gianni Dagli Orti/Historiska Muséet Stockholm/The Art Archive/Art Resource, NY, 16
© Ivy Close Images/Alamy, 8, 35, 36
© Keystone-France/Gamma-Keystone via Getty Images, 74
© Marvel/Paramount/The Kobal Collection/Art Resource, NY, 82
© Mary Evans Picture Library/Alamy, 42, 64
© Mary Evans Picture Library/The Image Works, 15
© Michael Nicholson/Corbis, 84
© Nationalmuseum, Stockholm, Sweden/The Bridgeman Art Library, 79
© North Wind Picture Archives/Alamy, 13
© Performance Image/Alamy, 67
© Photo Researchers, Inc., 45, 46, 52
© Stan Pritchard/Alamy, 24
© Timm Schamberger/AFP/Getty Images, 76
© Tom Lovell/NGS Image Collection/ The Art Archive/Art Resource, NY, 21
© Trevor Booth Photography/Alamy, 58
© Werner Forman/Art Resource, NY, 19, 31, 32
© Werner Forman/Corbis, 54
© Werner Forman/Courtesy of the Royal Commission on Historical Monuments/Art Resource, NY, 37

ABOUT THE AUTHOR

Shirley-Raye Redmond is the author of several nonfiction books for children, including *Mermaids, The Jersey Devil,* and *Blind Tom: The Horse Who Helped Build the Great Railroad.* Redmond lives in New Mexico. Visit her website at www.ShirleyRaye Redmond.com